Introduction

Social life has always been one of the greatest instigators of people wanting to sing together. And conversely, singing together often assists in making for a healthy social life. It is hoped, therefore, that this collection of songs, in accompanying children from age 8 through 14, will serve the social life of the classroom as much as the education of each individual. It is dedicated to all colleagues and pupils who may find it useful, in the hope that usage may lead to enjoyment, and that enjoyment may lead to many significant musical discoveries.

Ideally, in Waldorf Schools, the class-teacher accompanies his or her group of children for eight years, having received them at age 6. He or she is responsible for teaching run-of-the-mill subjects such as maths and English (or the mother tongue), history and geography, and many others besides.

Although there will probably be a music specialist on the staff, it usually also falls to the class-teacher to introduce simple songs as part of the daily activities at the beginning of or during the main lesson.

This selection has been made with that particular task in mind, though it may well be that teachers of English as a foreign language, or others, will find it a useful resource.

The songs are broadly 'graded' section by section so that the pupils and teacher can take them in their musical stride. They are mostly in keys that lend themselves to recorder-playing, which is also a common activity in Waldorf as well as other schools. In later years, other instruments may well be brought in as support, particularly for the part-songs. The grading is naturally only a guide and is intended to be taken in that spirit.

These songs are meant to stand on their own melodic ground

without the use of any accompaniment, even though (as in Gluck's "Che farò senza Euridice", for instance) several have important accompaniments in the original. This is not to imply that someone with the neccessary ability should not add an appropriate accompaniment, either by reference to the full score, by improvising, or by devising something that the pupils themselves could manage.

At the same time, a certain stress has been laid on rounds, which (apart from in the Notes) have not been differentiated from canons, and simple part-songs from age 9-10 upwards. The range of difficulty offered should make it possible for all classes to experience the creating of harmony together.

The other categories into which the songs fall are:

Firstly, songs, whose subject may be associated with the suggestions that Rudolf Steiner made for the Waldorf curriculum. Into this category fall: "Ein feste Burg" (history of the Reformation); "The whirling mill" (farming); "Sigurd and the dragon" (Norse mythology) and many others.

Secondly, songs in foreign languages, particularly those languages not normally taught in schools — for instance, Sanskrit, Manx, Quechan, and so on. This acknowledges, at least in token, the wealth of culture that the whole of mankind has contributed towards. It is particularly important to cultivate such an attitude in our present-day multi-ethnic society.

Thirdly, a few samples in each section of well-known songs from one background or another, such as "The Skye Boat Song", Milton's "Let us with a Gladsome Mind" to the tune "Monkland"; amongst the rounds and "Come Follow, Follow," "Shalom Chaverim" and Byrd's "Non Nobis Domine".

Fourthly, there are also songs in each section which stem from the work of the Waldorf movement itself. These often arise from the specific need of a group. That they could be included here is gratefully acknowledged.

As in recitation, so in singing, one of the greatest needs of the teacher is for material that reflects the mood of nature, season by season, culminating often in one of the major religious festivals. This is recognized in the present edition insofar as the structure of each section begins with autumn/Michaelmas. It is hoped that teachers in the southern hemisphere will find that particular orientation acceptable.

Contents

The Waldorf Song Book

The Waldorf Song Book

Collected and edited
by Brien Masters

Floris Books

Music handwritten by Jenny Wellman
Illustrations by Astrid Maclean

First published in 1987 by Floris Books

Photocopying

Photocopying this book instead of buying it makes
future books more expensive, and robs those
who have put work into this book of their due.

Do not photocopy unless you have a licence or the
written permission of the publisher.

British Library CIP Data

The Waldorf song book.
1. Children's songs
I. Masters, Brien
784.6'2406   MI992

ISBN 0-86315-059-4

Printed in Great Britain
by the Camelot Press, Southampton

In the earliest part of the song book, the tempo and expression indications for each song are in English, except for the more obvious *p, f, cresc,* and so on. From age 10-11 the usual Italian terminology is then gradually introduced as part of the pupil's general music education.

One technicality needs to be clarified. Rounds are such that the usual sign for a pause is irrelevant (⌢). Where this sign is found over a note in any of the rounds, therefore, it indicates the point during the round where each voice should stop singing in order to synchronize the ending. As round singing is very familiar today, it is hoped that this will be sufficient guidance for teachers.

Finally, I would like to draw attention to the Notes. These are not at all scholastically exhaustive, but are intended to give teachers ideas for introducing the songs.

Brien Masters

Songs

Age 8-9
(Class 3)

1. Step We Gaily
Lewis Bridal Song

Joyfully

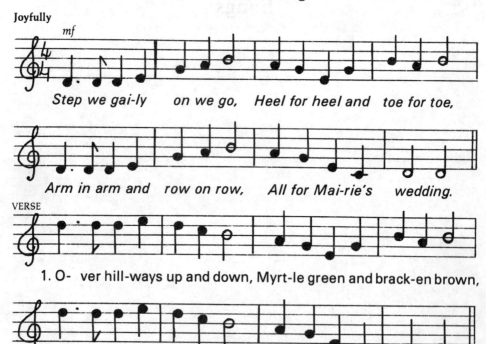

Step we gai-ly on we go, Heel for heel and toe for toe,

Arm in arm and row on row, All for Mai-rie's wedding.

VERSE

1. O- ver hill-ways up and down, Myrt-le green and brack-en brown,

Past the shielings through the town, All for Mai-rie's wed-ding.

2. Red her cheeks as rowans are
   Bright her eye as any star
   Fairest of them all by far
   Is our darling Mairie.

3. Plenty herring, plenty meal,
   Plenty peat to fill her creel,
   Plenty bonny bairns as weel,
   That's our toast for Mairie.

2. Unconquered Hero of the Skies

Michaelmas Song

With firmness

1. Un-con-quer'd he- ro of the skies, Saint Mi- cha-el———

——— ; A- gainst the foe with us a- rise, *Thine aid we pray the*

foe to slay, Saint Mi——————cha-el———.

2. The heavenly banner thou dost bear, Saint Michael;
   The angels do thine armour wear;
   Thine aid we pray the foe to slay, Saint Michael.

3. Great is thy might, strong is thy hand, Saint Michael;
   Great o'er the sea, great o'er the land;
   Thine aid we pray the foe to slay, Saint Michael.

3. Green Lies the Dancing Water

Smoothly

Green lies the danc-ing wa-   Green, pur-ple barr'd with gold;

Brown wing'd my boat flies o'er her,   Brown wing'd, while

out   the wa-ter; White the keel, the   curl- ing wave-let

crescendo   *diminuendo*

toss-   es   high,   spray- ing round ——————.

4. Heaven Blue

Not too fast

1. Heav-en blue, clothe a-   new, light in dark- ness
2. Sing-ing star,   near and   far, Shades of si- lence

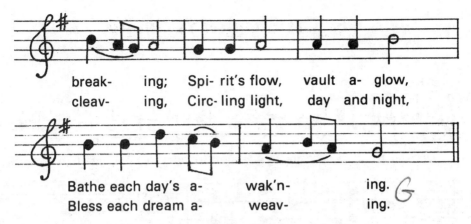

break- ing; Spi- rit's flow, vault a- glow,
cleav- ing, Circ- ling light, day and night,

Bathe each day's a- wak'n- ing.
Bless each dream a- weav- ing.

Music reproduced by permission of Bärenreiter Verlag, Kassel

5. Let Us with Gladsome Mind

With a strong rhythm

Let us, with a glad-some mind, Praise the Lord for he is kind:

For his mer-cies ay en-dure, E- ver faith-ful, e- ver sure.

2. Let us blaze his name abroad,
   For of gods he is the God:
   For his mercies ay endure,
   Ever faithful, ever sure.

3. He with all-commanding might
   Filled the new-made world with light:

4. He the golden tressèd sun
   Caused all day his course to run:

5. The hornèd moon to shine by night,
   'Mid her spangled sisters bright:

6: All things living he doth feed,
   His full hand supplies their need:

7. Let us, with a gladsome mind,
   Praise the Lord, for he is kind:

15

6. The Shepherd's Song

Lightly

Once upon a starry midnight Stood I up-on a mountain Silver-grey the silent sheep

Slumbering, slumbering, Slumbering so deep, A- mong the hills so fair.

2. Quietly the vault above me
   Opened like the rose in summer:
Rainbow light streamed through its
   crown
     Glimmering, glistening,
     Jewelling all down
   Among the hills so fair.

3. Winging through the midnight
     splendour
   Angels with chanting voices,
Songs of joy and songs of birth
     Carolling, carolling:
     Joy to all the earth,
   Among the hills so fair.

4. Gladly then I turned my footsteps
   Down to the straw-bright cradle;
There I danced with heart-filled glee,
     Merrily, merrily,
     Merry-merrily,
   Among the hills so fair.

Words from *Weft for the Rainbow* by permission of Lanthorn Press.

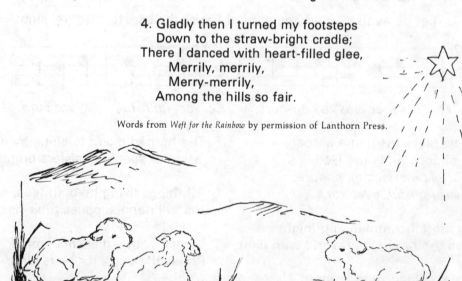

7. Skye Boat Song

With a gentle lilt

Speed, bon-ny boat, like a bird on the wing,

"On-ward" the sail-ors cry. Car-ry the lad that's

born to be king, O- ver the sea to Skye. Skye

1. Loud the winds howl, loud the waves roar,
2. Though the waves leap, soft shall ye sleep,

Thun-der-claps rend the air. Ba-ffled our foes
O-cean's a roy- al bed. Rock'd in the deep,

stand by the shore, Fol- low they will not dare. *(Chorus)*
Flo- ra will keep Watch by your wea-ry head. *(Chorus)*

8. The Whirling Mill

With movement

mf

The whirling mill goes blithely round, goes blithely, blithely round,

I love to hear its bu-sy sound, its bu- sy, bu- sy sound

I love to mark a-gainst the blue Its white arms swinging; two and two,

Its dome with shadowy fan- tail crowned————————.

meno moso

Its feet are firm in earthen mound, Its bulk with oaken beams in-bound,

It stands erect where all may view The whir- ling mill.

tempo primo

And facing windward straight and true, straight and true,

It does the work it finds to do, it finds to do,

The wheat, the barley, sun-embrown'd, To white & snowy meal are ground,

ritardando

And ho! the wind sings blithe- ly through————

The whirl- ing mill.

9. On this, our Glorious Eastertide

With a broad rhythm

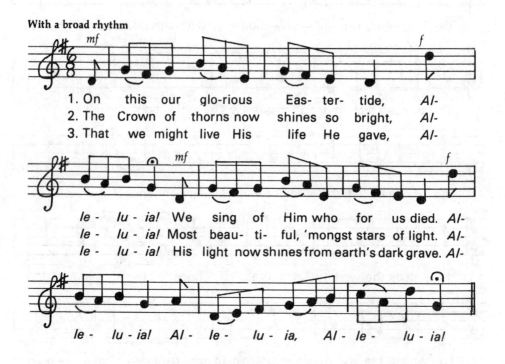

1. On this our glo-rious Eas-ter-tide, Al-
2. The Crown of thorns now shines so bright, Al-
3. That we might live His life He gave, Al-

le - lu - ia! We sing of Him who for us died. Al-
le - lu - ia! Most beau-ti-ful, 'mongst stars of light. Al-
le - lu - ia! His light now shines from earth's dark grave. Al-

le - lu - ia! Al - le - lu - ia, Al - le - lu - ia!

10. This Joyful Easter Day

Radiantly

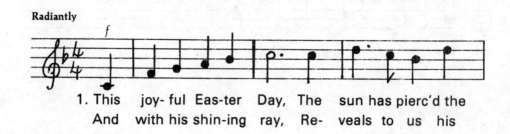

1. This joy-ful Eas-ter Day, The sun has pierc'd the
And with his shin-ing ray, Re- veals to us his

clouds of night ——————— ;   And   like the seed that
wond-rous light ——————— .

grows from ev'r-y   flow'r that dies ——————— ;   More

ra-diant than the   rose.   Let   love   in Man a-

- rise ——, a - rise ——, a - rise ——, Let

love   in Man a - rise ————————————— .

2. The corn is milled for bread
   Grain glowing once, in glowing sun;
   Each deed on earth a thread,
   That may in web of life be spun.
      (Chorus)

3. *The grape is pressed for wine;*
   The broken branch sends forth a shoot;
   The jewel lies in the mine;
   The hollow reed becomes a flute.
      (Chorus)

11. Over the Hills and Far Away

Easily flowing

1. Tom he was a pi-per's son, He learn'd to play when
2. Tom with his pipe made such a noise, That he pleas'd both the

he was young; But all the tune that he could play Was
girls and boys; And so they stopp'd to hear him play———:

CHORUS

"O- ver the hills and far a-way". O- ver the hills and a

great way off, The wind shall blow my top-knot off.

12. The Dawn Wind now is Waking

A Béarnaise Summer Carol

Gently

1. The dawn wind now is wak-ing, Round go the windmill's

22

arms, And sun on sha-dow break-ing Lights up the shel-ter'd

farms.   Un-der   cows the milk-maids crouch-ing In the

mists of morning grow;   Boys with   heavy   horses slouching Down to

wa-ter lum-ber   slow; Grey as   rocks the strag- gling

sha-d'wy flocks With   si-lent shep-herds   go.

2. Now quickly goes the grey light;
   A-slant, the sun redeems
   A whole long day of daylight;
   Gold crowd a wealth of beams.
   Chickens flutter, strut and babble;
   Running ducks the duck-pond fill;
   Early breezes bear the gabble,
   And the light increases till
   Soon it finds beyond the rabble
   The blackbird's yellow bill.

3. Bright flow'rs the woods adorning
   Show earth's no longer blind,
   As once on Christmas morning,
   When snow the world did bind,
   When the shepherds and the sages
   And the kings first met their King,
   Brought him wisdom, wealth, and wages
   Though he was the littlest thing;
   Suddenly the iron ages
   Had yielded to the spring.

English words from the *Oxford Book of Carols* by permission of Oxford University Press

13. Little Red Bird of the Lonely Moor

Manx Lullaby

Tenderly

Ush-ag veg ruy ny moan-ee doo, Moan-ee doo,

moan-ee doo, Ush-ag veg ruy ny moan-ee doo. O

where did you sleep last night? 1. Out on a gorse-bush
2. Did I not sleep on a

dark and wide, Dark and wide, dark and wide, Swift the rain
sway-ing briar, Sway-ing briar, sway-ing briar, Toss-ing a-

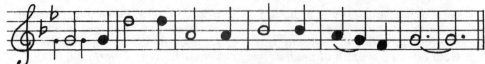

fell on ev' -ry side, My sleep was hard last night.
-bout as the wind rose high'r, My sleep was hard last night.

(Chorus)
3. Did I not sleep on a cold wave's crest,
Cold wave's crest, cold wave's crest,
Where many a man has taken his rest?
My sleep was hard last night.

(Chorus)
4. Wrapped in two leaves I lay at ease,
Lay at ease, lay at ease,
As sleeps the young babe on its mother's knees
My sleep was sweet last night.

14. Down in the Valley

Austrian Shepherd's Song

With rustic gaiety

mf 1. Down in the val- ley where sum- mer's laugh-ing beam
f 2. Ah, how they strug-gle, and pant, the sil- ly sheep,
p 3. Eve- ning is o- ver the land, with peace and light,

Un- der the wil- low tree lights a- long the stream,
Fear-ing the hands that dip, fear- ing wa- ter deep.
Now sits the shep-herd a- lone in eve- ning bright,

Shep-herds come driv- ing their flocks and seek the pool,
Ten- der -ly lift- ed up, glad- ly, one by one,
Now has he joy with-in, where he pi- peth low,

Plung-ing their sheep in the sun- ny wa- ter cool.
White in the green of the mea- dow, lo, they run.
See- ing his flock gath-er'd round him white as snow.

Words from the *Oxford Book of Carols* by permission of Oxford University Press

15. How Beautiful they are, the Lordly Ones

Unhurriedly and with attention to the broad phrasing

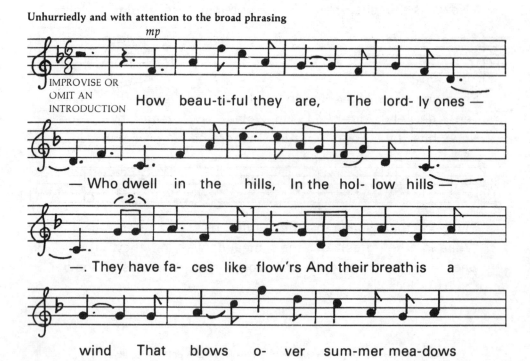

IMPROVISE OR
OMIT AN
INTRODUCTION

How beau-ti-ful they are, The lord- ly ones —

— Who dwell in the hills, In the hol- low hills —

—. They have fa- ces like flow'rs And their breath is a

wind That blows o- ver sum-mer mea-dows

Fill'd with dew-y clo- ver. Their

limbs are more white than shafts of moon- shine,

They are more fleet than the March wind, They

laugh and are glad and are ter- ri - ble

When their lan-ces shake and glit-ter Ev' ry green reed qui-vers.

How beau-ti-ful they are, How beau-ti-ful——

——The lord- ly ones in the hol-low hills.

16. How Delightful to See

A Sheep Shearing Song from Somerset

Simply and happily

1. How de- light- ful to see, In those eve-nings in spring, The sheep go-ing home to the fold: The mas-ter doth sing, As he views ev-'ry- thing, And his dog goes be- fore him where told ————, And his dog goes be-fore him where told —.

2. The sixth month of the year,
In the month callèd June
When the weather's too hot to be
    borne,
The master doth say,
As he goes on his way——:
"Tomorrow my sheep shall be shorn,
Tomorrow my sheep shall be shorn."

3. Now the sheep they're all shorn,
And the wool carried home;
Here's a health to our master and
    flock;
And if we should stay
Till the last goes away,
I'm afraid 'twill be past twelve
    o'clock. (*Repeat* I'm afraid ...)

17. Once on a Bright Summer's Day

Quickly, but not breathlessly

1. And once up-on a time on a bright sum-mer's
2. And when the sum-mer fad- ed and dark was the

day, I saw two boys and a lamb at
land Those two stood to- geth-er on Jor-dan's

play; Our little Je-sus and St John A- way into the
strand; With waters blue as heav'ns above, On hov'ring wings there

fields they've gone; One car- ries a por-rin- ger in his
came the dove; While John baptiz'd Jesus, came God's voice so

hand, As they walk through the clo- ver and but-ter-cup land.
free: "This day have I be- got- ten Thee."

18. The Ash Grove

Llwyn On (Welsh)

Very tunefully

1. The ash grove how grace-ful, how plain-ly 'tis
1. Yn Mhal-as Llwyn On gynt, fi drig-ai pen-

speaking, The wind thro' it play-ing has lan-guage for
def-ig, Ef e oedd ys- gwei-ar ac ar- glwydd y

me; When o- ver its branches the sunlight is breaking, A
wiad; Ac idd-o un en-eth a an-wyd yn un-ig, A

host of kind fa- ces is gaz-ing on me. The
hi 'nol yr han- es oedd aer-es ei thad. Aeth

friends of my child-hood a- gain are be- fore me, Fond
Car- iad i'w gwel-ed, yn idn a phar lenc-yn, Ond

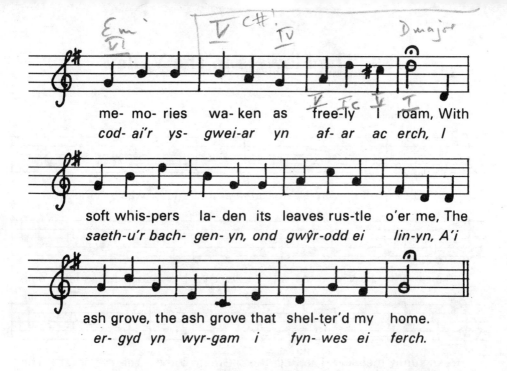

me- mo- ries wa- ken as free-ly I roam, With
cod- ai'r ys- gwei-ar yn af- ar ac erch, I

soft whis-pers la- den its leaves rus-tle o'er me, The
saeth-u'r bach- gen- yn, ond gwŷr-odd ei lin-yn, A'i

ash grove, the ash grove that shel-ter'd my home.
er- gyd yn wyr-gam i fyn- wes ei ferch.

2. My laughter is over, my step loses lightness,
    Old countryside measures steal soft on mine ear;
I only remember the past and its brightness,
    The dear ones I mourn for again gather here.
From out of the shadows their loving looks greet me,
    And wistfully searching the leafy green dome,
I find other faces fond bending to greet me:
    The ash grove, the ash grove alone is my home!

2. *Rhy hwyr ydoedd galw y saeth at y llinyn,*
    A'r llances yn marw yn welw a gwan;
Bygythiodd ei gleddyf trwy galon y llencyn;
    Ond ni redai Cariad un fodfedd o'r fan.
'Roedd Golud, ei "darpar" yn hèn ac anynad,
    A geiriau diweddaf yr Aeres hardd hon,
Oedd, "gwell genyf farw trwy ergyd fy Nghariad
    Na byw gyda Golud yn Mhalas Llwyn On."

19. The Flowers in the Valley

With a steady rhythm

1. O there was a wo- man and she was a wid- ow,

Fair are the flow'rs in the val- ley, With a daugh-ter as fair as a

fresh sunny meadow, The Red, the Green, & the Yel- low. The

harp, the lute, the pipe, the flute, the cymbal, Sweet goes the treble vi-o-

-lin: The maid so rare and the flow'rs so fair, To-

-geth- er they grew in the val- ley.

2. There came a knight all clothed in red,
     Fair are the flowers in the valley;
    "I would thou wert my bride," he said,
     The Red, the Green, and the Yellow.
   The harp, the lute, the pipe, the flute, the cymbal,
     Sweet goes the treble violin:
   "I would," she sighed, "ne'er wins a bride!"
     Fair are the flowers in the valley.

3. There came a knight all clothed in green,
     Fair are the flowers in the valley;
    "This maid so sweet might be my queen,"
     The Red, the Green, and the Yellow.
   The harp, the lute, the pipe, the flute, the cymbal,
     Sweet goes the treble violin:
   "Might be," sighed she, "will ne'er win me!"
     Fair are the flowers in the valley.

4. There came a knight, in yellow was he,
     Fair are the flowers in the valley;
    "My bride, my queen, thou must with me!"
     The Red, the Green, and the Yellow.
   The harp, the lute, the pipe, the flute, the cymbal,
     Sweet goes the treble violin:
   With blushes red, "I come," she said;
     "Farewell to the flowers in the valley."

20. Waken Sleeping Butterfly
Birthday Song

With a rocking rhythm

1. Wa- ken sleep- ing but- ter- fly, Burst —
2. Birth- day sun break through the clouds, Shine —

— your nar- row pri- son;
— on joy and sor- row;

Spread your gol - den wings and fly
Life and light for earth to- day;

For the sun has ri - sen.
Star of love to- mor - row.

21. The Merry Haymakers

Flowing happily

1. The gol-den sun is shin- ing bright, The

dew is off the field; To us it is our main de-light The fork and rake to wield.

The pipe and ta- bor both shall play, The vi- ols loud- ly ring, From morn till eve each sum-mer day, As we go hay- mak- ing.

2. As we, my boys, haymaking go,
   All in the month of June,
   Both Tom and Bet, and Jess and Joe,
   Their happy hearts in tune.
   Oh up come lusty Jack and Will,
   With pitchfork and with rake,
   And up come dainty Doll and Jill,
   The sweet, sweet hay to make.
   The pipe and tabor ...

3. Oh when the haysel all is done,
   Then in the arish grass,
   The lads shall have their fill of fun,
   Each dancing with his lass.
   The good old farmer and his wife
   Shall bring the best of cheer,
   I would it were, aye, odds my life!
   Haymaking all the year.
   The pipe and tabor ...

Age 9-10
(Class 4)

22. Sigurd and the Dragon
A Faeroese Folk Song

Strong and firm

English translation from *Folk Songs of Europe* by permission of Maud Karpeles and Novello & Co Ltd.

1. Come, good peo-ple, lis-ten now, Lis-ten to my sto-ry
2. It was Si-gurd brave and bold, Rode the heath of Glit-ra.

Of the rich and migh-ty kings And their deeds of glo-
'Gainst the one who meets his sword He will show no pi-

-ry. Gra- ni brought gold from the heath O. Gra-
-ty.

-ni bar gull av hei- di. Brá hann si- num bran-

-di av rei- di. Si- gurd struck the dra- gon dead.

Gra- ni bar gul- lid av hei- di!

3. On the gold the dragon lies,
   Shrieking loud in vengeance.
   Sigurd sits on Grani's back,
   With his sword he threatens.
      Grani brought gold from the heath O.
   (Alternative English words:)
      Gold from the heath he brought O,
   Swung his sword with rage and anger.
      Sigurd struck the dragon dead.
   Swung his sword with rage and with anger.

4. Sigurd gave so big a thrust,
   'Twas a mighty wonder;
   Trembled both the leaves and trees
   As though struck by thunder. (*Chorus*)

5. It was Sigurd brave and bold,
   He his sword did brandish;
   In two parts asunder lay
   Dead the glitt'ring dragon. (*Chorus*)

23. Happy Birthday

A Round in Three Parts

With a light, happy motion

Hap- py birth-day, hap- py birth-day, Many, many happy re-

-turns; Hap- py birth-day, hap- py birth-day

Sun and moon and stars re- joice Upon your birthday, upon your

birth-day, While we join hands in a ring and sing:

24. Reap the Flax

Swedish Reaping Song

Vigorously

1. Come, har-vest now the ripe flax to- day, Card, card it well, and spin, spin a-way.
2. Come, now the flax we're card-ing to- day, Card, card it well, and spin, spin a-way.

Soon we will weave our costumes so gay, Then off we go a- danc-ing.
Soon we will weave our costumes so gay, Then off we go a- danc-ing.

Doonk, doonk, doonk, doonk, doonk, doonk, Spools whirl a-round, spools whirl a-round.

Doonk, doonk, doonk, doonk, doonk, doonk, Then off we go a- danc- ing.

3. Come, now the flax we're spinning today,
   Carded so well, we spin, spin away.
   Soon we will weave our costumes so gay,
   Then off we go a-dancing.
   Doonk, doonk, etc.

4. Now finest cloth we're weaving today,
   Spinning is done, we weave, weave away
   Soon we will weave our costumes so gay,
   And lightly swing in dancing,
   Doonk, doonk, etc.

25. The Frosty Air is Echoing

A Huntsman's Song

Rousing but not rowdy

1. The fros- ty air is e- cho-ing with bu- gle clear the
   The king and all his fol- low-ers are rid- ing forth to

   live- long day, *All the merry woods are glad To*
   seek their prey. *Of the horses' pounding hoofs Up-*

   hear the sound For soon no more The wild boar Will
   on the ground,

   ra- vish tra- vel- lers on their way.

2. Against the bare black forest trees
   The hunting coats are bright and gay:
   With loping stride and panting breath
   The blood-hounds bring their beast to bay.
   All the merry woods are glad
   To hear the sound
   Of the horses' pounding hoofs
   Upon the ground,
   For soon no more
   The wild boar
   Will ravish travellers on their way.

3. Come, come, mine host pile high the fire!
   Let's see the flames and shadows play,
   For while it burns the hunt returns —
   Out in the court the horses neigh.
   (Chorus)

4. With utmost care the grooms attend
   In stable sweet with new-spread hay,
   And round the board both king and knight
   Their lordly manners now display.
   (Chorus)

26. Alleluia

A Round in Three Parts

With purity and fullness of tone

Al- le - lu - ia, al- le- lu- ia, al-le-lu-ia,

Al- le - lu - ia, al- le- lu - ia, al-le-lu-ia,

Al- le-lu- ia, al- le- lu- ia, al- le- lu- ia, al- le- lu- ia.

27. The Song of Christmas Day

A Round in Three Parts

With buoyancy

Come and join in the song of Christ- mas Day;

An- gels are throng-ing on their way; Shep-herds are danc-ing;

Hear their round-e-lay Of love for the babe who lies in the hay.

28. New Year

A Round in Four Parts

In broad, sweeping phrases

mf

New Year,   New Year,   What will you   bring?

1. Haste & hurry,   work & worry, *All are on the   wing:*
2. Noughts & crosses, gains & losses,
3. Sun & shower,   seeds & flower,
4. Laughing, weeping, sowing, reaping,

With   a   ding-dong,   ding-dong,   ding-dong,

Ding-dong,   ding,   ding, dong,   ding.

29. Where is John?

A Round in Three Parts

Rhythmically bouncing

Where is   John? The   old red hen has   left her pen.

Where is   John? The   cows are in the   corn a-gain, O

John ——————————————————————————————.

30. To Wander is the Miller's Joy

A Song by Schubert

At a convenient pace

1. To wan-der is the   mil-ler's joy To   wan- der

To   A   sor- ry mil-ler he must be Who

nev-er wan-der'd far   and   free And   wan-der'd,   and

wan-der'd, And   wan-der'd,   and   wan-der'd.

2. The water 'twas that taught us this, the water, *(repeat)*
   That day or night no rest has known,
   And still must wander on and on,
   The water, the water ...

3. We learn it from the mill-wheels too, the mill-wheels, *(repeat)*
   They turn all day with right good will
   And love not to be standing still,
   The mill-wheels, ...

4. The millstones, too, for all their weight, the millstones, *(repeat)*
   They dance along in merry mood
   And would go quicker if they could,
   The millstones, ...

5. To wander is my only joy, to wander, *(repeat)*
   O master mine and mistress dear,
   Bid me no longer tarry here,
   But wander, and wander,
   But wander, and wander.

English translation reproduced by permission of Oxford University Press

31. Love is Come Again

With a steady, confident flow

1. Now the green blade ris- eth   from the bur-ied grain,
2. In the grave they laid him, Love whom men had slain,

Wheat that in the dark earth ma- ny days has lain;
Think- ing that nev- er he would wake a- gain,

Love lives a- gain, that with the dead has been:
Laid in the earth like grain that sleeps un- seen:

Love is come a- gain, Like wheat that spring-eth green.

3. Forth he came at Easter, like the risen grain,
   He that for three days in the grave had lain,
   Quick from the dead my risen Lord is seen:
   Love is come again, ...

4. When our hearts are wintry, grieving, or in pain,
   Thy touch can call us back to life again,
   Fields of our hearts that dead and bare have been:
   Love is come again, ...

Words and music from the *Oxford Book of Carols* by permission of Oxford University Press

32. A Sea-Bird to her Chicks

A Gaelic Song

Quickly, but distinctly   The words in the *italic* transliteration are pronounced as the familiar English ones.

Each- ak- an each- ak- an   oo- een
I - teag-an I - teag-an   ubh- uin

Each- ak- an each-ak-an yawn   Each-ak-an each- ak- an
I - teag-an I - teag-an eòin   I - teag-an I - taeg-an

oo- een,   Shèh mo nee-an   a nee kyòl Thou'll thou'll
ubh- uin   'Sè mo nigh-ean   a ni ceòl Dall Dall

jay- re- room oh Thou'll jay-ree room o ro   Thou'll thou'll
der- i- rum o Dall der- i- rum o ro   Dall dall

jay- ree room oh Shèh mo nee- an   a nee kyòl
der- i- rum o 'Sè mo nigh-ean   a ni ceòl

Each- ak- an each- ak- an   oo- een!
I - teag-an I - teag-an   ubh- uin!

45

33. Tomorrow Shall be my Dancing Day

Broadly, with a feeling of one beat in a bar

1. To- mor-row shall be my danc-ing day: I would my
2. For thir- ty pence Ju- das me sold, His co- vet-

true love did so chance To see the le-gend of my
ous-ness for to ad- vance;"Mark whom I kiss, the same do

play, To call my true love to my dance:
hold,"The same is he shall lead the dance:

Sing O my love, O my love, my love, my
love; This have I done for my true love.

3. Before Pilate the Jews me brought,
   Where Barabbas had deliverance;
   They scourged me and set me at
       nought,
   Judged me to die to lead the dance:
   Sing O my love ...

4. Then on the cross hangèd I was,
   Where a spear to my heart did
       glance;
   There issued forth both water and
       blood,
   To call my true love to my dance:
   Sing O my love ...

5. And as the sun, in chariot gold,
   Was dulled, like knight unhorsed by
       lance,
   The earth did quake, the rocks were
       rent
   Beneath the trembling of the dance.
   Sing O my love ...

6. Then down to hell I took my way
   For my true love's deliverance,
   And rose again on the third day,
   Up to my true love and the dance:
   Sing O my love ...

7. With spices rare they came at morn
   But stood amazed, as in a trance,
   When they beheld the stone rolled
       back,
   To set me free to lead the dance.
   Sing O my love ...

8. In raiment white my angel stood,
   Like lightning was his countenance,
   Whereat the keepers shook with
       fear,
   Dead to my true love and the dance.
   Sing O my love ...

9. Then in the garden I appeared
   My love's new dawning to enhance;
   In upper room, on sandy shore
   I led the gathering Easter dance.
   Sing O my love ...

10. Then up to heaven I did ascend,
    Where now I dwell in sure substánce
    On the right hand of God, that man
    May come unto the general dance:
    Sing O my love ...

34. Kookaburra

An Australian Round in Three Parts

With clearly accentuated rhythm

Koo- ka- bur- ra sits on an old gum- tree;

Mer-ry, mer-ry king of the bush is he;

Laugh, Kookaburra, laugh; Kookaburra, gay your life must be.

35. Bells Ring, Rise and Sing

A Finnish Melody

At a moderate speed

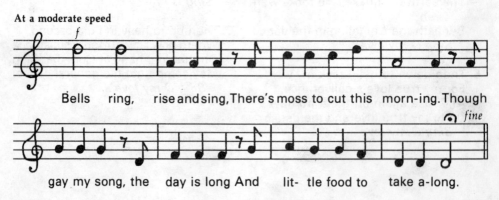

Bells ring, rise and sing, There's moss to cut this morn-ing. Though

gay my song, the day is long And lit- tle food to take a-long.

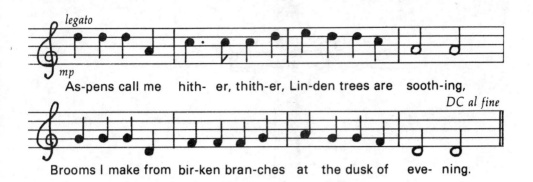

legato

mp

As-pens call me hith- er, thith-er, Lin-den trees are sooth-ing,

DC al fine

Brooms I make from bir-ken bran-ches at the dusk of eve- ning.

36. O Soldier, Won't you Marry me?

Briskly

mp

"O soldier, soldier, won't you marry me, With your musket, fife and drum?" "Oh

fine　*mf*

no, sweet maid, I cannot marry thee, For I have no 1.coat to put on!" Then
　　　　　　　　　　　　　　　　　　　　2. hat 3. gloves 4. boots
　　　　　　　　　　　　　　　5. For I have a wife of my own!"

up she went to her grandfather's chest And got him a 1. coat Of the very, very best, She
　　　　　　　　　　　　　　　　　　　　　　　2. hat
　　　　　　　　　　　　　　　　　　some 3. gloves 4. boots

got him a 1. coat Of the very, very best, And the soldier put it on.
　　　　　　　2. hat
　　some 3. gloves 4. boots　　　　　　　　　　　　　　　them

49

37. I Bind unto Myself Today

St Patrick's Hymn

Broad, firm, and with conviction

1. I bind un- to my- self to- day The strong name of the Tri- ni- ty, By in- vo- ca- tion of the same, The Three in One, and One in Three.

2. I bind un- to my- self to- day The vir- tues

3. I bind un- to my- self to- day The pow- er of

of the star- lit hea-ven, The glo- rious
God to hold and lead, His eye to

sun's life- giv- ing ray, The white- ness of the
watch, his might to stay, His ear to heark- en

moon at ev'n, The flash- ing of the light- ning
to my need. The wis- dom of my God to

free, The whir- ling wind's tem- pes-tuous shocks, The
teach, His hand to guide, his shield to ward; The

sta- ble earth, and deep salt sea, A-
word of God to give me speech, His

-round the old e- ter- nal rocks.
heav'n- ly host to be my guard.

38. In the Red of Evening

Tenderly and with sustained tone

Oh how fair this world of thine, Fa-ther, in the sun-set
Bask-ing in thy gaze di- vine, Ev-en dust to beau-ty

burn- ing,
turn- ing When the clouds are chang'd to shades of rose

and my west- ern win-dow glows. Gone is weep- ing

fled is sor- row, Now I feel thy pre- sence near. Then se-

-rene will dawn to- mor-row, Pa-ra- dise is here be- low,

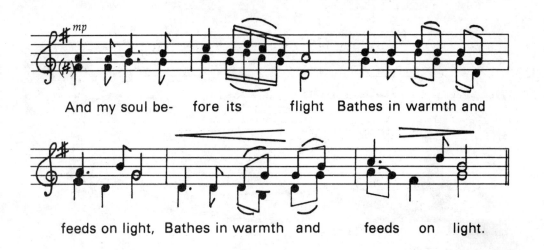

And my soul be- fore its flight Bathes in warmth and

feeds on light, Bathes in warmth and feeds on light.

39. We've Ploughed our Land

A Clapping Round in Three or Four Parts

Quickly, but not skating over the notes

We've plough'd our land, we've made all neat and gay,
we've sown our seed,

So take a bit and leave a bit, a- way birds, a- way.

Shoo ah oh shoo ah shoo oh.

CLAP

40. For all the Saints

Vaughan Williams

With breadth, but without dragging

For all the saints who from their la-bours rest

Who thee by faith be- fore the world con- fest, Thy

name, O Je- sus, be for e- ver blest:

Al- le- lu- ia, al- le- lu- ia.

Words and music reproduced by permission of Oxford University Press

41. Alleluia for all Things

A.C. Harwood

1. Of all created things, of earth and sky,
   Of God and man, things lowly and things high,
   We sing this day with thankful heart and say,
   Alleluia, alleluia.

2. Of light and darkness and the colours seven
   Stretching their rainbow bridge from earth to heav'n,
   We sing this day ...

3. Of sun and moon, the lamps of night and day,
   Stars and the planets sounding on their way,
   We sing this day ...

4. Of times and seasons, evening and fresh morn,
   Of birth and death, green blade and golden corn,

5. Of all that lives and moves, the winds ablow,
   Fire and old ocean's never-resting flow,

6. Of earth and from earth's darkness springing free
   The flowers outspread, the heavenward reaching tree.

7. Of creatures all, the eagle in his flight,
   The patient ox, the lion that trusts his might,

8. Of Man, with hand outstretched for service high,
   Courage at heart, truth in his steadfast eye,

9. Of angels and archangels, spirits clear,
   Warders of souls and watchers of the year

10. Of God made man, and through man sacrificed,
    Of man through love made God, Adam made Christ,

42. Iduna

Slowly and sadly

Sor-row, sor-row, va- nish'd is I- du- na.

Lone-ly, lone-ly droops the Tree of Life.

Cold-ly, cold-ly, blows the wind of win-ter.

Sor-row, sor-row, va-nish'd is our queen.

43. Bugles Gaily Call us

A Round in Four Parts

Energetically

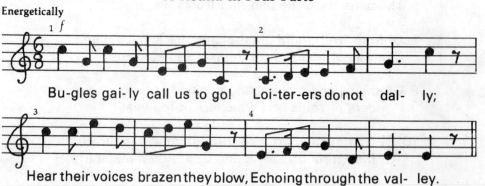

Bu-gles gai-ly call us to go! Loi-ter-ers do not dal- ly;

Hear their voices brazen they blow, Echoing through the val- ley.

44. Glory to Thee, my God, this Night

A Canon in Eight Parts

Evenly without being rushed

1. Glo- ry to thee, my God, this night For all the bless-ings of the light; Keep me, Oh keep me, King of Kings, Be- neath thine own al- migh- ty wings.

2. Oh may my soul on thee repose,
   And with sweet sleep mine eyelids close,
   Sleep that may me more vig'rous make
   To serve my God when I awake.

3. Praise God, from whom all blessings flow;
   Praise him, all creatures here below;
   Praise him above, ye heavenly host;
   Praise Father, Son, and Holy Ghost.

45. Clouds of Rain

A Round in Four Parts

In a simple, natural manner

Clouds of rain, blue a-bove; Eas-ter sun and Whit-sun dove.

Age 10-11

(Class 5)

46. Life from Dead Furrow

A Danish Harvest Song

Allegro *mf*

1. Life from dead fur- row, by plough-share once rif- ted;
High on the corn- rick, the ripe grain is lif- ted;

Sharpen'd scythes and swishing swathes, the har-vest time now starts;
Jogg-ling on the wa- gon: ti- red limbs but sing-ing hearts.

mp

Sun of the sum-mer's height, Brings us strength for win-ter's plight;

f

Loaves are bak- ing; Mer- ry mak- ing; Join the har-vest song.

2. So will be garnered the harvest of ages;
Present, past, and future, whether bringing love or strife;
Thought, word and action; both monarch and pages;
All the little things that fill the round of daily life.
Sun of the summer's height ...

47. When Autumn Mists Gather

A Round in Three Parts

When au-tumn mists gath- er And leaves fall gently down; New strength in me ri- ses To bear life's waiting crown.

48. Bhajan

He Bha-ga- van ta- ru nam, Sam bla-la-to ra-hu sa-gha- le- tam; Ga-ga- ne pa-va-ne va-ne up-a-va-na-re; Kha-la kha-la jha-ra- ne ta- ru gan.

Sing in the traditional manner: slowly at first; then repeat faster, and a third time still faster; finally slowing right down the fourth time.

49. Hail Light of Lights

Sanskrit

Andante con moto

mp

Jos- ti sham, Jos- ti

shay, Na-ma-ha, na-ma- ha, na-ma- ha

50. The Fire of Ash Twigs

Andante cantabile

mp

Cold was the sta- ble, Wild was the storm;

"Light a fire, my Jo-seph, that our child may be warm."

Jo-seph with his lan-tern went out in- to the night;

Jo-seph brought in branch-es, but none could he light.

On-ly the green ash twigs   Jo-seph did not try: "How

can I kin-dle sap wood if I   can-not kin-dle dry?"

"Try the ash twigs, Jo-seph,   Green though they are. " The

ash twigs kin-dled like a leap- ing star. The

ash twigs kin-dled like a glow- ing sun.

"Now a sap of sun-light   In the ash shall run;

O-ther trees shall kin- dle on- ly when dead, But

ash shall kin-dle green or dry," the young child said.

51. Sanctus

A Round in Five Parts

Sanct————————us, sanct————
————us, sanct————————————
————————us, sanct————————us.

52. O Holy Night

A Round in Four Parts

O ho- ly night, with stars in the sky,

Where- in the Child of Heav'n was born;

Midst choirs of an- gels full of joy, winging their way,

Turn- ing the dark-ness into dawn.

CELLOS OR MEN'S VOICES (OPTIONAL)

53. Three Kings Come Star-led Riding

A Round in Three Parts

Con moto non tropo

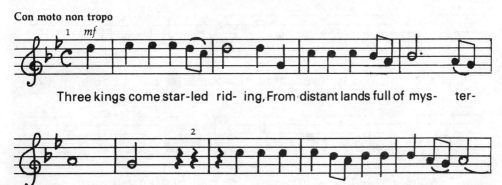

Three kings come star-led rid- ing, From distant lands full of mys- ter-

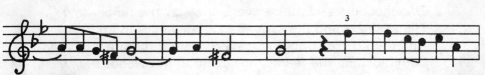

-y old; To seek, to seek out a king is their in- tent

—, a king of won- der un- told; They come to the child of

Mary mild, And give him their myrrh, frankin-cense and gold.

54. Come all ye Jolly Shanty Boys

A Canadian Lumbering Song

1. Come all ye jol-ly shan-ty boys, and lis-ten to my song. It's

all a-bout the shan-ties, and how they get a- long. They

are a jol- ly crew of boys, so mer-ry and so fine, Who

while a-way the win- ters, a- cut-ting down the pine.

2. The choppers and the sawyers, they lay the timber low
The skidders and the swampers, they holler to and fro.
And then there come the loaders, before the break of day,
Come load up the teams, boys, and to the woods away.

3. The broken ice is floating, and sunny is the sky,
Three hundred big and strong men are ready, wet or dry
With cant hooks and with jam pikes, these noble men do go
And risk their lives each springtime, on some big stream you know.

55. Blow the Wind Southerly

A Northumbrian Song

Lento semplice

Blow the wind southerly, southerly, southerly, Blow the wind south o'er the
Blow the wind southerly, southerly, southerly, Blow bonny breeze my

bon-ny blue sea. 1. They told me last night there were ships in the offing, and
lo-ver to me.

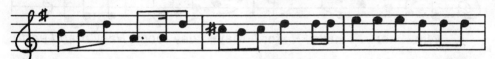

I hur-ried down to the deep rolling sea. But my eye could not see it wher-

-ev-er might be it, The bark that is bearing my lov-er to me.

2. Blow the wind southerly, southerly, southerly,
   Blow bonny breeze o'er the bonny blue sea.
   Blow the winds southerly, southerly, southerly,
   Blow bonny breeze my lover to me.
   Is it not sweet to hear the breeze singing,
   As lightly it comes o'er the deep rolling sea?
   But sweeter and dearer by far when 'tis bringing,
   The bark of my true love in safety to me.

56. Farewell Night

Andante

1. Fare- well night with mists o'ershrouded, Fare- well star and twi-light gloom; Wel-come sun-shine un- be-cloud-ed; Win- ter make for May- day room! *Heav'n and earth,* *Isle and o- cean, Frith and firth, Sing for mirth.*

2. Gold bright sun of spring's new morning
   Rising o'er the crests of hills,
   Dance now in thy robes of splendour
   While the Easter clarion trills. (*Chorus*)

3. Earth's fair mantle green and glistening,
   Soften'd by the April show'rs
   Burgeon forth to great Life's Hero
   Yield your ransom'd scent and flow'rs. (*Chorus*)

57. Easter Day

Allegro giocoso

mf *(f)*

1. The world it-self keeps Eas-ter Day, & Eas-ter larks are sing- ing; And Eas-ter flow'rs are blooming gay, And Eas-ter buds are springing; Al- le- lu- ia, al- le- lu- ia: The Lord of all things lives a- new, And all his works are *f* ris- ing too, *In no- va ju- ven- tu- te.*

2. There stood three Maries by the tomb,
   On Easter morning early;
   When day had scarcely chas'd the
      gloom,
   And dew was white and pearly:
   Alleluia, alleluia:
   With loving but with erring mind,
   They came the Prince of Life to find,
      Cum pia servitute.

3. But earlier still the angel sped,
   His news of comfort giving:
   And "Why," he said, "among the dead
   Thus seek ye for the living?"
   Alleluia, alleluia:
   "Go, tell them all, and make them blest,
   Tell Peter first, and then the rest,"
      Mandatum hoc secute.

58. Ye Banks and Braes o' Bonny Doon

1. Ye banks and braes o' bon-ny Doon, How can ye bloom sae fresh and fair! How can ye chaunt ye lit- tle birds, and I sae wea- ry fu' o' care! Ye'll break my heart, ye warb-ling birds that war- ble on the flow'r-y thorn, Ye 'mind me o' de- par- ted joys, de-par- ted ne-ver to re-turn.

59. St Francis' Hymn

At the speed of measured speech

1. O most high almighty good Lord God. To thee belong
praise, glory, honour, and all bless-ing.

2. Prais-èd be my Lord   and specially our brother
God, with all his creatures: the sun who brings us
the day and who brings us the light.

3. Fair is he, and
shining with a ve-   ry great splen-dour: O Lord, he signifies to us thee.

4. Prais-èd   be my Lord for our   sis- ter   the   moon,
5. Prais-èd   be my Lord for our   bro- ther the   wind,

and for the stars, the which he has set clear and love-ly in hea-ven.
and for air and cloud, calms, and all weather by
the which thou upholdest in   life all creatures.

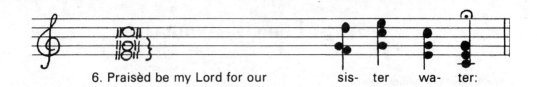

6. Praisèd be my Lord for our sis- ter wa- ter:

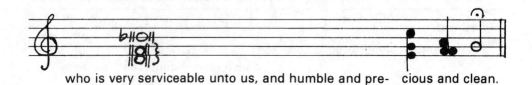

who is very serviceable unto us, and humble and pre- cious and clean.

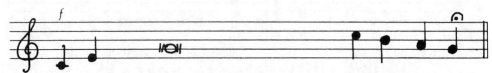

7. Prais-èd be my Lord for our brother fire,
through whom thou givest us light in the dark-ness:

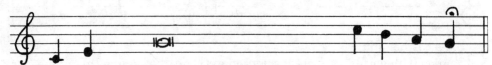

8. Prais-èd be my Lord for our mother the earth,
the which doth sustain us and keep us;

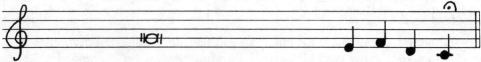

(7) and he is bright and pleasant and very migh- ty and strong.
(8) and bringeth forth divers fruit, and flowers of many co- lours, and grass.

9. Praisèd be my Lord
for all those who for his love's sake; and who endure
pardon one another weakness and tri- bu- la- tion.

10. Blessèd   are they
    who peace-
        ably   shall en-dure;

For thou, O
most Highest,
shalt   give them a crown

11. Prais-èd be my Lord for our sister the death   of   the   bo- dy:

blessèd are they who are found walking by thy most   ho-   ly   will.

mf

12. Praise ye   and bless ye the Lord and give   thanks un- to him:

f cresc

and serve him with   great hu-mi- li- ty.   Al- le- lu- ia, al- le- lu- ia!

60. Come Follow

A Round in Three Parts

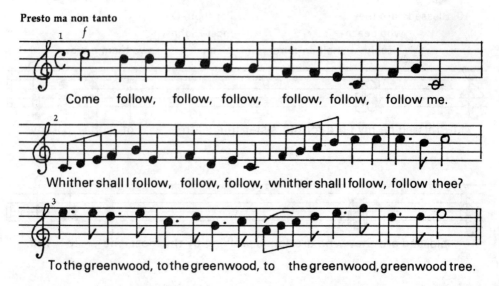

Come follow, follow, follow, follow, follow, follow me.

Whither shall I follow, follow, follow, whither shall I follow, follow thee?

To the greenwood, to the greenwood, to the greenwood, greenwood tree.

61. Che Farò Senza Euridice?

An Italian Song from Gluck's "Orfeo"

Che fa- rò senza Eur- i- di- ce, do-ve an-

-drò senza il mio ben? Che fa- rò do- ve an-

-drò che fa- rò sen- za il mi- o

ben do- ve an- drò sen- za il mi- o

ben? Eur-i- di- ce Eur-i- di- ce O

Di- o ri- spon- di ri- spon———

———di; io son pu- re il tu-o fe- de- le son

pu- re il tu-o fe- de- le il tu-o fe- de- le.

62. Good Friends When Gathered Together

A Round in Four Parts

Good friends when gather'd to-gether, Sing for the joy of sing-ing;

No mat- ter what the weather; Good friends are happy to-gether.

63. On the Hills the John-Fires Burn

A Round in Six Parts

Temp giusto

On the hills the John-fires burn; Flickering flames now leap and turn;

Hand in hand we all ad-vance To seek the warmth & join the dance; Rise,

too, my soul, en- dur-ing light, And, flame-like, burn for e- ver bright.

64. Migildi Magildi

A Welsh Folk Song

Con moto

When the sea comes o'er the moun-tains, *Mi-gil-di, ma-gil-di,*

hei, now now; When the de-sert flows in foun-tains,

Mi-gil-di, ma-gil-di, hei now, now, When ripe ap- ples

grow on this- tles, *Mi- gil- di, ma- gil- di,*

hei now, now; Oh then I'll come when

Da- vid whis-tles, *Mi- gil- di ma-gil- di, hei now, now.*

2. When the winter's bright in May-time, *Migildi ...*
When the stars shine in the day-time, *Migildi ...*
When from earth to heaven takes seconds, *Migildi ...*
Oh then I'll wake when David beckons. *Migildi ...*

English translation reproduced by permission of Oxford University Press

65. Glorious Apollo

A Part Song by Samuel Webbe

Allegro moderato

Glo- rious A- pol- lo from on high be- held us,

Wan-d'ring to find a tem-ple for his praise,

Sent Po- ly- hym- nia hith- er to shield us,

While we our- selves such a struc-ture might raise,

Thus then com- bin- ing, Hands & hearts join- ing

Sing we in har- mo-ny A- pol- lo's praise.

66. Sleep, Refreshing

A Round in Three Parts

Poco lento

Sleep, re- fresh-ing life a- new; Sun spark-ling in the crys- tal morn-ing dew; Tasks of life ful- fill- ing, stead-fast, pur- sue.

67. Greensleeves

Andante cantabile

1. A- las, my love, you do me wrong To cast me off dis-cour-teous-ly, And I have lov- éd you so long, de- light- ing in your com- pa-ny.

piu forte

Green-sleeves was all my joy, Green- sleeves was
my de-light, Greensleeves was my heart of gold, And
who but my la- dy Green-sleeves. Green-sleeves.

LAST TIME

2. I have been ready at your hand
   To grant whatever you would crave,
   I have both wagéd life and land,
   Your love and goodwill for to have,
       Greensleeves was all my joy,
       Greensleeves was my delight,
       Greensleeves was my heart of gold,
       And who but my lady Greensleeves.

3. I bought three kerchers to thy head,
   That were wrought fine and gallantly,
   I kept thee both at board and bed,
   Which cost my purse well favour'dly.
       Greensleeves ...

4. Well I will pray to God on high
   That thou my constancy mayst see,
   And that yet once before I die
   Thou wilt vouchsafe to love me.
       Greensleeves ...

Age 11-12
(Class 6)

68. Michaelmas Time
A Festive Song

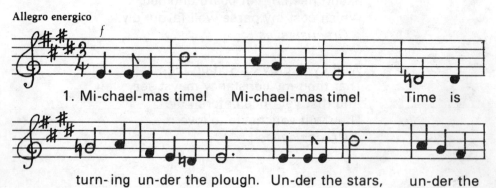

1. Mi-chael-mas time! Mi-chael-mas time! Time is turn-ing un-der the plough. Un-der the stars, un-der the

signs, The ploughman toils with deep furrow'd brow. He

turns his thoughts a-gainst the cold, Buries his fears 'neath the

earth's deep mould; Frost, like fire, burns white on the

blade of his i- ron share that red fire made.

2. Michaelmas time! Michaelmas time!
   Time is bending over the scales.
   Over the bread, over the wine,
   The ploughman bows his head at the rail.
   He turns his thoughts towards the flame,
   Raises his eyes to the thanksgiven grain;
   Stars, like spears, gleam over the tower
   Of the House of God in Michael's hour.

3. Michaelmas time! Michaelmas time!
   Time is changing the guard of the world.
   Deep in his heart, dauntless in mind,
   The ploughman guards against time growing old.
   He stands and studies the star-patterned sky,
   Fixes each spark in his wishing-well eyes:
   Stars, like seeds, strewn over the land
   And under the plough by Michael's hand.

69. Sunrise is Flaming

A Round in Three Parts by Cherubini

Allegro non troppo

Sun-rise is flam-ing, New morn pro- claim-ing;

Night's shades dis- pel- ling, Dawn cho- rus swel- ling;

Voi- ces and hearts rise to greet the day, Sun-rise is

flam- ing, New morn, new morn pro- claim- ing;

Night's shades dis- pel- ling, Dawn cho-rus swel- ling;

Voi-ces and hearts rise to greet the day,

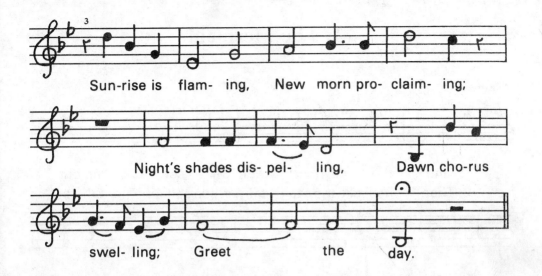

Sun-rise is flam- ing, New morn pro- claim- ing;

Night's shades dis- pel- ling, Dawn cho-rus

swel- ling; Greet the day.

70. Deo Gratias

A Round in Four Parts

Moderato cantabile

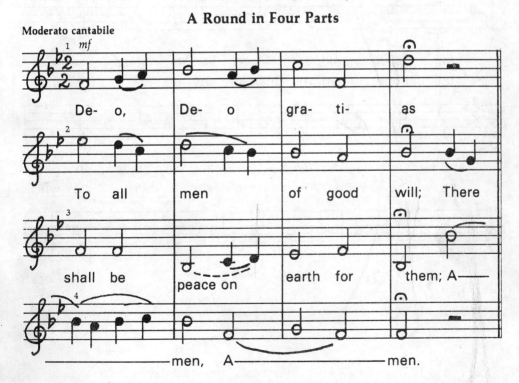

De- o, De- o gra- ti- as

To all men of good will; There

shall be peace on earth for them; A——

——men, A————men.

71. The Mermaid

Allegro vivo

1. One Fri- day morn, when we set sail, And our
2. Then up spoke the cap- tain of our gallant ship, Who at

ship not far from land, We there did es- py a
once did our per-il see, "I have mar-ried a wife in

fair pret-ty maid, With a comb and a glass in her
fair London town, And this night she a wi- dow will

hand, her hand, her hand, With a comb and a glass in her
be, will be, will be, And this night she a wi- dow will

hand. *While the ra- ging seas did roar, And the*
be". *For the*

storm-y winds did blow, And we, jol-ly sailor boys, were

up, up a- loft, And the land lub-bers ly- ing down be-

-low, be-low, be-low, And the landsmen were all down be- low.

3. And then up spoke the little cabin boy,
   And a fair hair'd boy was he;
   "I've a father and mother in fair Portsmouth town,
   And this night they will weep for me, for me, for me,
   And this night they will weep for me. *For the ...*

4. Then three times round went our gallant ship,
   And three times round went she;
   For the want of a life-boat they both went down,
   As she sunk to the bottom of the sea, the sea, the sea,
   As she sunk to the bottom of the sea. *For the ...*

72. Make We Merry

Rhythmically taut

CHORUS

mf

Make we mer-ry, both more and less, For now is the time of Chris- së-mass. Make we mer-ry, both more and less, For now is the time of Chris-së-mass.

mp

1. Let no man come in- to this hall, Groom, nor page, nor yet mar-shall, But that some sport he bring with all, For now is the time of Chris- së- mass.

REPEAT CHORUS

mp

2. If that he say he can- not sing, some other sport then

let him bring, That it may please at this feast-ing, For

now is the time of Chris- së- mass.

REPEAT CHORUS

73. Ring out, Wild Bells

Allegro moderato con sonore   Alfred Tennyson (1809-92)

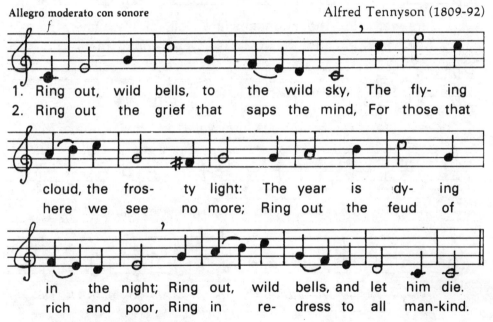

1. Ring out, wild bells, to the wild sky, The fly- ing
2. Ring out the grief that saps the mind, For those that

cloud, the fros- ty light: The year is dy- ing
here we see no more; Ring out the feud of

in the night; Ring out, wild bells, and let him die.
rich and poor, Ring in re- dress to all man-kind.

3. Ring out a slowly dying cause,
   And ancient forms of party strife;
   Ring in the nobler modes of life,
With sweeter manners, purer laws.

4. Ring out false pride in place and blood,
   The civic slander and the spite;
   Ring in the love of truth and right,
Ring in the common love of good.

5. Ring out old shapes of foul disease;
   Ring out the narrowing lust of gold;
   Ring out the thousand wars of old,
Ring in the thousand years of peace.

6. Ring in the valiant man and free,
   The larger heart, the kindlier hand;
   Ring out the darkness of the land,
Ring in the Christ that is to be.

74. Juvivalera

Allegro con spirito

1. Hol drain the bright wine cup. Hol sing with good cheer,
For the hour of our part- ing, my lov'd ones, is near.

Fare-well to the mountains, fare-well to my home; Fare-
My heart in the far world is yearn-ing to roam.

-well to the moun-tains, fare-well to my home; My

heart in the far world is yearn-ing to roam. Ju- vi

va- le-ra, ju- vi- va- le-ra, ju- vi- va- le-ra- le-ra- le-ra.

2. Not long doth the sun in his blue tent remain,
He flames o'er the ocean, he rolls o'er the plain;
The sea-wave grows weary of lapping the shore,
And the blasts of the tempests, how loudly they roar. *Juvivalera ...*

3. The bird on the white cloud is hurried along,
Afar doth it warble its home-loving song;
So speeds the young wand'rer through forest and fell,
Since his mother earth hasteth, he hasteth as well. *Juvivalera ...*

75. How Cool Blows the Breeze

Song from Weber's "Der Freischütz"

Molto vivace

1. How cool blows the breeze in the deep fo-rest glade   Where

In gol- den and rus- set they dance over all   And

leaves whisper soft-ly in sun-shine and shade.   A- bove the wide

gai- ly they carpet the ground where they fall.

branch-es and up to the skies. We see tow'ring moun-tains be-

-fore us a- rise, And then like the swal-lows that swift-ly de-

part, We haste to the hills with a joy-   ful heart.

2. Oh, sweet is the spell of the chill misty morn,
   The tall scented pines and the dew-studded dawn,
   And fresh is the stream as it sparkles so clear,
   What joy to be walking when autumn is here!
   Above the wide branches ...

76. When Winter Skies

A Song in Three Parts by Carl Loewe

Moderato

1. When win- ter skies are o- ver-cast & days are dark and
2. So when the storms of life grow dark, with need and
Threat'ning

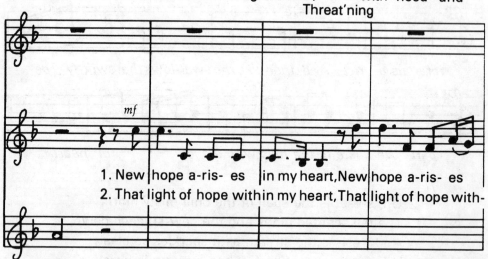

1. New hope a-ris- es in my heart, New hope a-ris- es
2. That light of hope within my heart, That light of hope with-

drear,
pain,

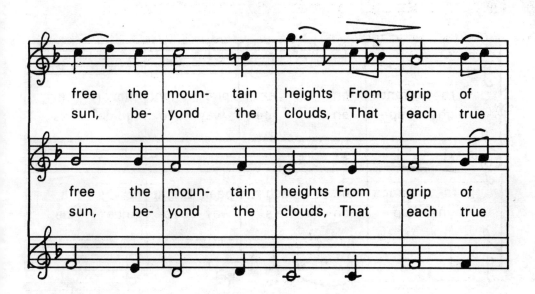

frost   and   ice;   In- to   its
pil- grim seeks   Will shed its

mp

frost   and   ice;   In- to   its
pil- grim seeks   Will shed its

mp

mp

ra- diance, on   each   peak, Bright flow'rs it
light up - on   life's   way To   guide   us

ra- diance, on   each   peak, Bright flow'rs it
light up - on   life's   way To   guide   us

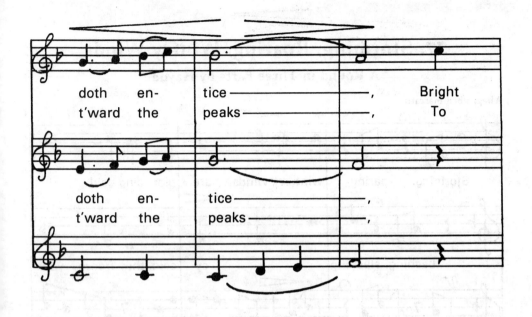

doth   en-   tice ——————— ,   Bright
t'ward   the   peaks ——————— ,   To

doth   en-   tice ——————— ,
t'ward   the   peaks ——————— ,

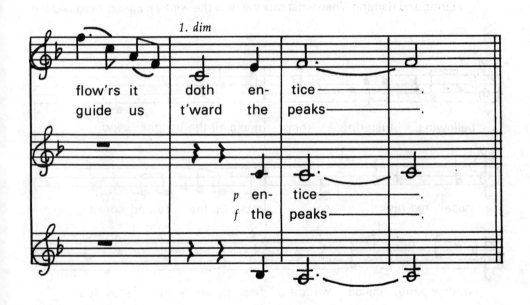

1. dim

flow'rs it   doth   en-   tice ——————— .
guide us   t'ward   the   peaks ——————— .

p en-   tice ——————— .
f the   peaks ——————— .

77. Storming, Roaring, Wintry Winds

A Round in Three Parts by Haydn

Allegro ben marcato

Storming, roaring, wint-ry winds are pier-cing cold;

Lashing, slashing i-cy cold, they freeze your

Flaring and flaming. Then what care we how the wintry twigs smite against the

bellowing, blustering they make all the boughs bend,

nose red raw; so stoke up the fire and set it

window pane: inside we are hap-py while out-side it's

78. Pange Lingua

Sing my Tongue the Glorious Battle

In a flowing, declamatory style

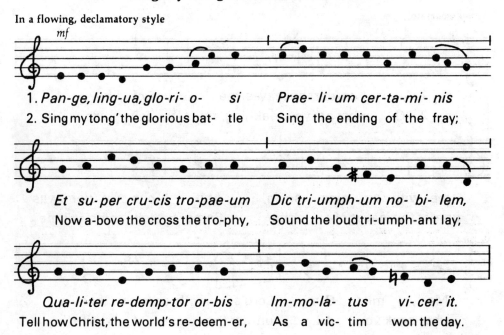

1. Pan-ge, ling-ua, glo-ri- o-   si   Prae- li- um cer-ta-mi- nis
2. Sing my tong' the glorious bat- tle   Sing the ending of the fray;

Et su- per cru-cis tro-pae-um   Dic tri-umph-um no- bi- lem,
Now a-bove the cross the tro-phy, Sound the loud tri-umph-ant lay;

Qua-li-ter re-demp-tor or-bis   Im-mo-la- tus   vi- cer- it.
Tell how Christ, the world's re-deem-er, As a vic- tim   won the day.

3. Noble Cross on Calv'ry lifted;
   From thy dead wood new life streams;
   Hope eternal rising ever,
   New-born sun from darkness gleams;
   Death's cold mouth acclaims the victor:
   Easter Lord the world redeems.

4. Pange, lingua, gloriosi
   (as verse 1, ad lib)

95

79. Under the Leaves of Life

Molto moderato

p

1. All un-der the leaves, the leaves of life, I
2. "O what are you seek-ing, you sev'n fair maids, All

met with vir-gins sev'n, And one of them was
un-der the leaves of life? Come tell, come tell me

Ma-ry mild, Our Lord's moth-er from heav'n.
what seek you All un-der the leaves of life."

3. "We're seeking for no leaves, Thomas,
  But for a friend of thine;
We're seeking for sweet Jesus Christ,
  To be our guide and thine."

4. "Go you down, go you down to yonder town,
  And sit in the gallery;
And there you'll find sweet Jesus Christ,
  Nailed to a big yew-tree."

5. "Dear mother, dear mother, you must take John,
  All for to be your son,
And he will comfort you sometimes,
  Mother, as I have done."

6. "O come, thou, John Evangelist,
  Thou'rt welcome unto me,
But more welcome than my own dear son,
  That I nursed upon my knee."

7. Then he laid his head on his right shoulder,
  Seeing death it struck him nigh:
"The Holy Ghost be with our soul;
  I die, mother dear, I die."

8. Oh the rose, the rose, the gentle rose,
  And the fennel that grows so green!
God give us grace in ev'ry place,
  To pray for our King and Queen.

80. Daffodils on Fields of Green

A Round in Four Parts

Andante piacevole

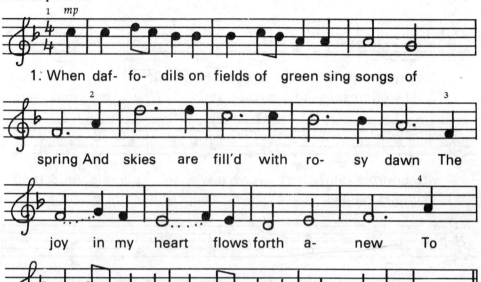

1: When daf- fo- dils on fields of green sing songs of
spring And skies are fill'd with ro- sy dawn The
joy in my heart flows forth a- new To
join in the song of gold and light that Christ is ris'n.

2. And thus it was on Easter morn the Maries came
   With hearts weigh'd down and tears of love,
   They made their way through the garden dew.
   The light of their life had set in depths of darkest night.

   3. "Oh who will roll away the stone?" in grief they cried,
      For deaf were they to lark and thrush,
      As near the sepulchre they came
      Wherein the body of the Lord was laid to rest.

4. But marvel rare! The stone roll'd back with mighty quake;
   Upon it sat the youth from heav'n,
   As white as snow was the robe he wore,
   Like lightning was his countenance, his forehead flame.

   5. With finger rais'd to heav'n he spake: "He is not here."
      Whereat the sorrow from their hearts
      Like stone from the tomb was roll'd away;
      "To Galilee, O fairest land, we make our way."

81. Why with Bulrush Mock Him?

Lento

1. Why, oh why with bul-rush mock Him? Of His own robe
2. Why on cross by thief e-rec- ted? Why de- nied and

poco a poco cresc

why un-frock Him? Thorn-crown'd, why in pur- ple smock Him?
un-pro-tec-ted? God's own Son, to this e- lec- ted?

Why, oh why with bul- rush mock Him?
Why de- nied and un- pro-tec- ted?

dim

mp

Why, oh why with bul- rush mock Him?
Why on cross by thief e- rec- ted?

3. Why unknown, the world's Redeemer?
Bound and scourged by harsh blasphemer?
Helpless He — of all, supremer?
Bound and scourged by harsh blasphemer?
Why unknown the world's Redeemer?

4. Easter sun will brim day's dawning;
Joy will follow night of mourning;
Vict'ry conquer hell's gate yawning;
Joy will follow night of mourning;
Easter sun will brim day's dawning.

82. The Streams in the Mountains

A Round in Three Parts

The streams in the mountains Are tumb-ling like fountains;

With yo- d'ling in the val-ley, And cow- bells in spring.

Fa- la-la- la-la- la-la- la——, Fa- la-la- la-la- la-la- la.

83. While the Flames Leap up

A Round in Three Parts

While the flames leap up, Merrily we all are sing- ing, sing-

-ing; Mer-ri-ly, mer-ri-ly, To our hearts new joy is bring- ing, bring-

-ing; Mer-ri-ly, mer-ri-ly, song & flames go skyward, Hearts in heaven.

84. Light Ever Gladsome

An Italian Three-Part Folk Hymn

Calmo

1. Light e-ver glad- some, of the e- ter- nal
2. Day-time is o- ver; sun-less is hea ven,

3. Son of the High- est, thou the Life- giv- er,

splen-dour su- per- nal, ho- ly and true,
Lamps of the e- ven glim-mer and shine:

Art now and e- ver wor-thy of praise:

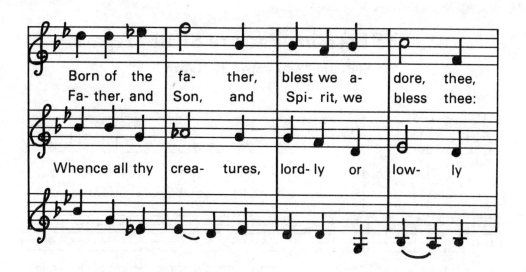

Born of the fa- ther, blest we a- dore, thee,
Fa- ther, and Son, and Spi- rit, we bless thee:

Whence all thy crea- tures, lord- ly or low- ly

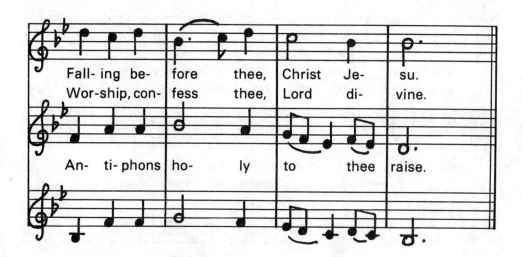

Fall- ing be- fore thee, Christ Je- su.
Wor- ship, con- fess thee, Lord di- vine.

An- ti- phons ho- ly to thee raise.

The dynamics of each verse should reflect the mood of the words.

85. The Lord my Pasture Shall Prepare

Psalm 23 to music by Haydn

Sereno

1. The Lord my pas- ture shall pre- pare, And
2. When in the sul- try glebe I faint, Or

feed me with a shep- herd's care; His pres- ence
on the thirs- ty moun-tain pant, To fer- tile

shall my wants sup- ply, And guard me with a
vales and dew- y meads My wear- y wand'- ring

watch- ful eye; My noon- day walks he shall at-
steps he leads, Where peace- ful ri- vers, soft and

-tend, And all my mid- night hours de- fend.
slow, A- mid the ver- dant land- scape flow.

3. Though in a bare and rugged way
Through devious lonely wilds I stray,
Thy bounty shall my pains beguile;
The barren wilderness shall smile
With sudden greens and herbage
    crowned.
And streams shall murmur all around.

4. Though in the paths of death I tread,
With gloomy horrors overspread,
My steadfast heart shall fear no ill,
For thou, O Lord, art with me still
Thy friendly crook shall give me aid,
And guide me through the dreadful
    shade.

86. Fie, nay prithee, John

A Round in Three Parts by Henry Purcell

Affretando

Fie, nay prithee, John, Do not quar-rel, man,

Let's be mer-ry and sing a song!

You're a rogue, you chea-ted me! I'll prove be-fore this com-pa-ny, Your

word's not worth a farth-ing, sir, you've done me wrong!

Sir, tut, tut, I scorn your charge, You are a lu- na- tic at large, So

eat your words, your temper keep, and go, go a- long!

87. The Veil of Destiny is Drawn

From Mozart's "Magic Flute"

Larghetto

The veil of des- ti- ny is drawn; The

path con-ceal'd ap-pears be- fore you: Take

cour- age now, as one new-born, De- vo- ted,

mind-ful and de- ter-min'd. A- lert with-in, stand

in the world, De- vo- ted, mind-ful and de-

-ter-min'd. On these de-pend: Pow'rs of your

soul; Till vict'ries ban- ner be for all un-furl'd.

soul; Till vict'ries ban-ner be for all un-furl'd.

Till vict'ries ban————ner be for all un- furl'd.

Till vict'ries ban-ner be for all un- furl'd.

88. Anne de Bretagne

A French Folk Song

Moderato

1. C'était Anne de Bre-tagne, duchesse en sa-bots,

Re-ve-nant de ses do- mai-nes, en sa-bots, mir- li- ton- tai-ne,

Ah————! Viv-ent les sa- bots de bois!

2. Entourée de châtelaines, avec ses sabots, (2)
   Voilà, qu'aux portes de Rennes, en sabots mirlitontaine
   Ah! Vivent les sabots de bois!

3. L'on vit trois beaux capitaines, avec ses sabots (2)
   Offrir à leur souveraine, en sabots mirlitontaine
   Ah! Vivent les sabots de bois!

4. Un joli pied de verveine, avec ses sabots (2)
   «S'il fleurit tu seras Reine» en sabots mirlitontaine
   Ah! Vivent les sabots de bois!

5. Elle a fleuri la verveine, avec ses sabots (2)
   Anne de France fut reine, en sabots mirlitontaine
   Ah! Vivent les sabots de bois!

89. Headstrong Horses on the Plain

A Hungarian Canon in Two, Three, Four or More Parts

Poco sforzato

mf

Headstrong horses on the plain, Gal-lop-ing to- geth- er;

Matted manes and flashing eyes, Tails as light as feath-er;

f

Pound-ing bare-back side by side, Wave on wave like

mp

surg-ing tide, O'er rock and spring-y heath- er;

mf *cresc (molto)*

LAST TIME

Foaming mouths and fly-ing turf, Sweating hell-for-leather, Hi!

SEE OVER FOR SINGING IN PARTS

89. Headstrong Horses (in parts)

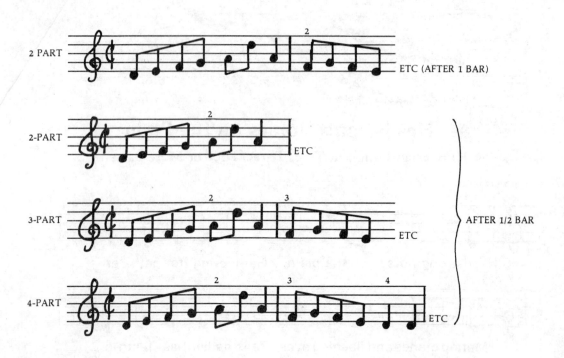

ETC (AFTER 1 BAR)

ETC

AFTER 1/2 BAR

ETC

ETC

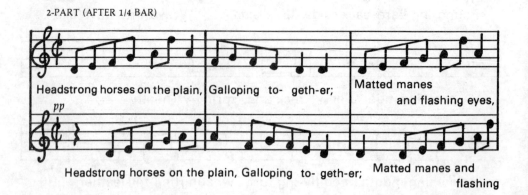

2-PART (AFTER 1/4 BAR)

Headstrong horses on the plain, Galloping to- geth-er; Matted manes and flashing eyes,

pp

Headstrong horses on the plain, Galloping to- geth-er; Matted manes and flashing

mf   *cresc*

Tails as light as feath-er; Pound-ing bare-back side by side,

eyes, Tails as light as feather; bare-back side by side,

Wave on wave like surg-ing tide, O'er rock and springy heath-er;

Foaming mouths and Sweating hell-for-leather, Hi!
fly-ing turf,
pp

Foaming mouths and turf, Sweating hell-for-leather, Hi!
fly-ing

3-PART 2 3   4-PART 2 3 4

AND SO ON TO EIGHT PARTS

109

Age 13 upwards

(Classes 7 and 8)

90. Michael Sea-Lord
A Celtic Song

Nobilmente

1. Mi-cha-el, Sea Lord, Shield of light! To-night a
2. Mi-cha-el, Sea Lord, Shield of light! To-night a

boat sets out to sea. Vel yoo, vel yoh, hoo-oo ran
child sets out to sea.

yay- li, yoo-vel yoh hoo hoh ran yay; Vel

yoo vel yoh hoo-oo ran- yay- li.

91. The Paths of Life are Steep

A Round in Three Parts by Haydn

Moderato energico

The paths of life are steep, The ways of life are long; They call for hu-man strength, For here we all be-long. Life's paths are steep, Life's ways are long. They call for strength, For here we all be-long. When paths are steep, When ways are long, When strength is need-ed, We be-long.

92. Firmly on the Earth I Stand

A Michaelmas Round in Three Parts with Ostinato Bass

On the slow side but with conviction

Firm- ly on the earth I stand; Mi-cha-el's sword with-

-in my hand; When I conquer fear, the dragon's chains I tightly bind;

Mi- cha-el's light with- in my mind; When I thrust a-

-gainst the monster's pride, Mi- cha- el is at my side.

OSTINATO

When I con-quer with-in me fear and wrath,

Mi- cha- el in heav'n casts the dra- gon forth. When I*

* The second group sings antiphonally, that is to say, dividing the mens voices into two groups, the first singing the part through once and then resting while the second group sings, and so on. The second group enters as indicated by the small notes in brackets.

93. Bubbling and Splashing

A Round in Three Parts by Henry Purcell

Tempo giusto

Bubb-ling and splash-ing and foam-ing and dash-ing with
noise and with bus-- tle the brook rush-es by, But
Si- lent and slow does the deep ri- ver flow On its
smooth glas-sy sur-face re- flect- ing the sky Thus
Shal-low pre- tence bub-bles on with-out sense while true
know-ledge and wis- dom sit si- lent-ly by.

94. Ein feste Burg

From the Reformation by Martin Luther

Ein fes- te Burg ist un- ser Gott, ein gu- te
Er hilft uns frei aus al- ler Not, die uns jetzt

Wehr und Waf- fen. Der alt bö- se
hat be- trof- fen.

Feind mit Ernst er's jetzt meint; gross Macht und viel List

sein grau-sam Rüst-ung ist, auf Erd' ist nicht seins glei- chen.

95. O God of Heaven, Hear my Praises

Lobgesang by Johann Sebastian Bach

Allegretto

1. O God of hea-ven, hear my prais- es;
2. In so- li- tude to Thee in- clin- ing

Deep in my soul Thy migh- ty strength I feel; Thy
We can ap- proach Thee in our dai- ly pray'r; And

glo- rious work my heart up- rais- es,
where the stars of heav-en are shin- ing

All Thy cre- a- tion doth Thy pow'r re- veal; When
In world ex- pan- ses, Thou art sure- ly there; Thy

Thou art by my side I fear not strife; In
guid- ing hand led man-kind in a- ges past, And

love to Thee I call, great Lord of Life.
Thou art with us now, un-to the last.

96. Who Will Come to the Sea

A Dutch Sea Song

Poco pesante

poco f　　　　　　　　　　　　　　　　　　*a piacere*

1. Who will come now with me to the sea?
2. Brave and strong, go we now to the sea! *Hold her fast now!*
3. Then we'll give three cheers for the sea!

tempo

Fresh blows the wind thro' furrows　free.　　You may
Rea-　dy to keep our country　free.　　With an
Men　of　Holland, shout with　me!　　For the

simile

stay　on　shore with the　rest,
eye　on the sail as　we　haul, *Hold her fast　now!*
sea　makes he- roes of　all,

Life　on the sea is still the　best!　　He who
Glad- ly　we heed our country's call!　Upward
On-　ly　the brave will heed her call!　In　a

fame would find　does not　stay be- hind,　No he
turn　our eyes　lest a　storm sur- prise;　We will
sea- man's breast, courage　still may rest;　In his

116

casts his lot with the sea, Finding for- tune free.
steer our swim- ming horse, Holding fast our course!
fist he holds his life, Fears but God in strife.

97. Never Weather-Beaten Sail

Thomas Campion

Andantino

1. Ne-ver wea-ther beat-en sail more will-ing bent to shore,
Ne-ver ti- réd pilgrim's limbs af- fec-ted slum-ber more

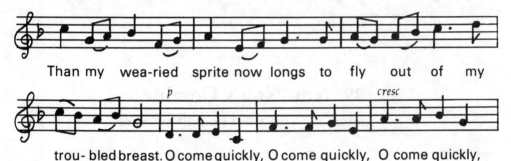

Than my wea-ried sprite now longs to fly out of my

trou- bled breast. O come quickly, O come quickly, O come quickly,

sweet-est Lord, and take my soul to rest.

2. Ever blooming are the joys of heav'n's high paradise.
Cold age deafs not there our ears, nor vapour dims our eyes;
Glory there the sun outshines, whose beams the blessed only see.
O come quickly, O come quickly, O come quickly,
Glorious Lord, and raise my sprite to thee.

98. Lord of the Universe, Hear my Prayer

Ancient Indian Chant

sempre f

Om bhur bhuv(a) sva-ha, Tat sav-i-

-tur va-ren- yam, Bhar go de- vag- ya di-ma-

-ni, Dyo-yo, na pra- cho- da- yat.

99. Non Nobis Domine

A Round in Three Parts by William Byrd

Cantabile

Non no- bis do- mi- ne non no- bis

mp

Non no- bis do- mi- ne non no-

mp

Non no- bis do- mi-

ALL THREE VOICES
FINISH TOGETHER
AT THE PAUSE
(ADJUST WORDS AD LIB)

119

100. Come and Sing this Christmas Morn

A Two or Three Part Polish Carol

Allegro vivace

1. Come and sing this Christmas morn,
Ra- diant shines the Christmas light

Come and sing, Come and sing, come and sing,
Radiant shines, radiant shines,

1ST TIME

2ND TIME

Of the Lord of earth now born;
Through the ho- ly

night.

Of the Lord of earth now born;
Through the ho- ly

night.

Come and sing your re- ve- la- tion; God's Son born for

ev'- ry na-tion: Glo- ri- a, Glo- ri- a

Glo-ria, Glo-ria

Glo- ri- a in ex- cel- sis De ——

Glo- ria in ex- cel- sis De ——

2. Shepherds dance and spread the fame,
That the angel choirs proclaim;
Holy night of Saviour's birth;
   Heaven born on earth.
Angels' errand, shepherds singing:
Men of good-will, peace now bringing.
   Gloria, Gloria,
   Gloria, in excelsis Deo.

101. The Crown of Roses

Tchaikovsky's "Legend"

Moderato

When Je-sus Christ was yet a child He had a gar- den

small and wild, Where-in he che-rish'd ro- ses fair,

And wove them in- to gar-lands there. Now once, as sum- mer-

-time drew nigh, There came a troop of chil-dren by,

And seeing ro- ses on the tree, With shouts they pluck'd them

mer- ri- ly. "Do you bind ro-ses in your hair?"

They cried, in scorn, to Je- sus there, The boy said humb-ly:

"Take, I pray, All but the nak- ed thorns a- way."

Then of the thorns they made a crown, And with rough fing-ers

press'd it down, Till on his fore-head fair and young, Red

drops of blood like ro- ses sprung.

English translation by G. Dearmer from the *Oxford Book of Carols* by permission of Oxford University Press

102. Taquiriri

A Bolivian Huanyo

1. Ta-qui-ri-ri ly- su nya-ni-tay, Tu-su-ri-ri ly- su-un.
2. Charangoy wag-ha-san nya-ni-tay, Si- mi-si-tuy man-ta a
3. Noghapis wag-ha- ni nya-ni-tay, Nya-wi-si-tuy man-ta a.

CHORUS

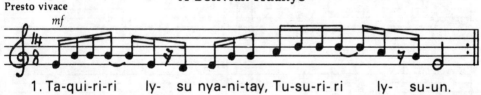

piu forte
Ay, chispa, chispa, nya- ni-tay, Lu-ri wanyu chispa a.

4. Ly ly ly ly ly ... etc.

103. I Gaze out o'er the Moonlit Earth

A Breton Carol

Andante meditativo

sotto voce

1. I gaze out o'er the moon- lit earth,

Hush'd still and sol- emn all a- round

The fros-ty air is keen and cold

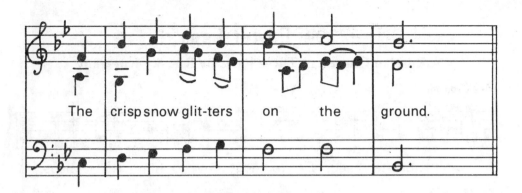

The crisp snow glit-ters on the ground.

2. So cold and sharp; and yet I know
   On such a winter night of old
   He came, the Holy Child, and lay
   In manger cradle, rude and cold.

3. O light, once born in earth's dark night
   Make bright for us the path we tread,
   Our hearts make warm with thy great love
   Until our souls to thee are led.

104. Easter Eggs

A Russian Chorus in Three Parts by Rimsky-Korsakov

2. To the poor, open the door;
   Something give of your store,

3. Those who hoard can't afford:
   Moth and dust their reward,

4. Those who love, freely give,
   Long and well may they live,

5. Eastertide, like a bride,
   Comes and won't be denied,

105. 'Neath the Spreading Chestnut Branches

A Round in Four Parts by Haydn

'Neath the spreading chestnut branches, Vil-lage folk are gay;

'Neath the spread of merry laughter, Greetings ring from floor to raf-ter

for the wedding day. Cheer up friends and cease your

moan- ing. Hear the spank-fat bagpipes dron-ing And the

white scrub'd
food-stack'd tables groaning; Cast care a- way!

Come in bright ar- ray. Take your part-ners for the

dancing; Fiddlers' elbows prancing; Join in the jig and skip in the fray;

Sweethearts singing, twist-ing, clap-ping, Plea-ted skirts and

ap- rons wild-ly flap-ping in the hey.

106. All Through the Night

Ar Hyd y Nos

Andante contenerezza

1. Fie- ry day is   e- ver mock-ing Man's fee-ble sight: Man's sight:
Dark-ness eve by   eve un- lock-ing Heav'n's cas-ket

1. Fie- ry   day is   e- ver mock-ing Man's fee-ble   sight: Man's sight:
Dark-ness eve by   eve un- lock-ing Heav'n's cas-ket

1. Fie- ry   day is   e- ver mock-ing Man's fee-ble sight ——————:
Dark-ness eve by   eve un- lock-ing Heav'n's cas-ket

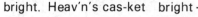

bright. Heav'n's cas-ket   bright ——————————————

bright. Heav'n's   casket   bright, the bur-den'd   spi-   rit bor-rows

bright ——————————. Thence the bur-den'd   spi-   rit bor-rows

.La- bo- rious mor- rows, Star-ry peace to

dim   *mf*

Strength to meet la- bo- rious mor- rows, Star- ry peace to

Strength to meet la- bo- rious mor- rows, Star- ry peace to

soothe his sor-rows, all through the night.

p   *dim*

soothe his sor-rows, all through the night————.

soothe his sor-rows, all through the night————.

2. Planet after planet sparkling
    All through the night,
Down on earth their sister darkling,
    Shed faithful light.
In our mortal days declining
    May our souls, as calmly shining,
Cheer the restless and repining,
    Till lost in sight.

107. Sumer is icumin in

A Round in Twelve Parts

Cheerfully

Sum-er is i- cum-en in, Lhu- de sing cuc- cu.

Groweth sed and bloweth med & springth the wu-de nu.

Sing cuc- cul Aw- e ble-teth af-ter lomb. Lhouth

af- ter cal- ve cu. Bul-luc ster-teth, buck-e ver-teth,

130

mu- rie sing cuc- cu!   Cuc-   cu,   cuc- cu,

wel sing-es thu cuc- cu: Ne swik thu na-ver   nu.

GROUND

Sing cuc- cu, nu,   sing cuc-   cu.   Sing   cuc-

ETC

Sing   cuc-   cu nu,   sing cuc-

ETC

108. Shalom Chaverim

Israeli Round in Four Parts

Allegro non tanto

Sha- lom chaverim! Sha-lom chaverim! Sha- lom, sha- lom!   Le-

heet-ra- ot, le- heet-ra- ot, sha- lom,   sha-   lom!

131

Notes

Age 8-9 (Class 3)

1. Lewis is one of the Hebridean Isles. In the second verse, there is reference to the rowan tree, which also figures in the legend of St Bride.

2. This song unites the text of a Michaelic song with a melody that is still within the ambit of the pentatonic.

3. A fairly wide-ranging song, evocative of the isles off the west coast of Scotland whence it derives.

4. This song, originally written for a christening, was inspired by an evensong.

5. The tune "Monkland" appeared in Manchester in 1824 at the time of and in the region of England's "dark, satanic mills". Milton wrote his words, it seems, in 1623, that is, as an adolescent. This was just before the headlong plunge into the scientific age — which was first taken in the British Isles — ushered in the Industrial Revolution. Words and music — two rays of light in a technologically brilliant, but in many aspects a fearsome, dark age.

6. Using only notes of the pentatonic scale, this melody lends itself to class improvisation with Orff-type instruments, such as glockenspiel, chime bars, and so on.

7. After his defeat in the Battle of Culloden in 1746, Bonnie Prince Charlie escaped to the Island of Skye off the north-west coast of Scotland.

8. These words were unearthed by the Sussex Archaeological Society, and reflect the unique relationship of earlier times between the human being and his daily work, almost personified, in this instance in the wind-mill.

9. There is implicit in the rhythm of this Dutch folk-song a dance-like quality, containing a heavy, cloglike two in a bar, and at the same time a strong, liberated, uplifting note of joy. These help to crystallize one important aspect of the Easter festival.

10. An important stream in the history of music, which was a significant tributary for J.S. Bach, was through the Dutch organist Adrian Willaert, who also had important Venetian connections. This fine tune was published in his home city, Amsterdam, in 1685, the year of Bach's birth. The words by Catherine van Alphen have been specially written for it.

11. This derives from the *Beggar's Opera* by John Gay of 1728 which achieved such popularity that even Handel's success in the London society of his day tremored on its musical pedestal. This simple ballad form appealed to the man in the street, presenting folk tunes, both native and foreign. Interestingly enough, it appeared just four years after the institution of the great Three Choirs Festival of Gloucester, Worcester and Hereford.

12. The delightful 2/4 bars that intervene in this tune from Béarnaise (south-west France) give it a distinct, unrigid character, Geoffrey Dearmer's words capture all the freshness of dawn, as if he had painted a few strokes with the brush of a Cuyp or a Hobbema.

13. The desolation of the peat moor and the ruggedness of the Isle of Man landscape, as well as its noble beauty, echo in the modal melody of this folk song.

14. There is a decided Tyrolean touch about this folk melody, that rides very happily in tandem with Laurence Binyon's description of the sheep being dipped.

15. The "Immortal Hour" by Rutland Boughton (1878-1960) was performed at Glastonbury during the summer festival of August 1914. Though never intended to be pretentious, it was hoped that a renewal of Arthurian culture would be brought about through its inception.

16. Folk song has attracted the attention of the so-called music world since the end of the eighteenth century. The resurgence of interest caused by Cecil Sharp and his associates has brought untold riches to many lives.

17. Raphael's and other Renaissance painters' work abound in depictions of the two cousins Jesus and John. Seldom do they appear in literature. This exception is inoffensively naïve. The second verse was added for use at St John's Tide — interestingly enough a celebration of birth, not of martyrdom.

18. Never more happily expressed, this song provides an example of the Welsh natural gift for music. The bardic tradition is still underestimated in many circles, but has been brought more into public awareness recently.

19. The colourful imagery of this folk song together with its gloriously free melody have endeared it to generations of children.

20. This song was written by Tom Scratchley for a young class in Edinburgh in order to celebrate birthdays in the classroom in a fresh and lively manner.

21. This haymakers' song comes from the West Country, an area rich in cattle farming, and carefully cultivated pastures and meadows on various soils, ranging from the Cheddar region in the north, down to the red sandstones of Devon.

Age 9-10 (Class 4)

22. The Edda is at the root of northern culture. It is often considered as being more refined than the equivalent mythological source used by Wagner in his Ring. In this song, Sigurd's slaying of the dragon is recounted to a folk melody of tremendous power.

23. In Waldorf Schools, rounds and part-singing are begun at this age. A birthday round can often be a welcome addition to the class repertoire.

24. Flax, from field to wardrobe, takes much hard labour and delicate skill. This traditional song describes some of the processes.

25. The royal forests in many parts of the British Isles gave rise to many woodland crafts. This song first appeared under the title "A Song of Anderida", referring to one of the longest remaining of the forests in the Wealden area of south-east England. Its theme, the overcoming of the wildness of nature, has inner connotations.

26. This round, by virtue of its 6/4 tempo builds up into an experience of musical circling. This is also evident in Botticelli's *Mystic Nativity* where the angelic host circles over the stable and the events below.

27. The jollity of the shepherds after the Nativity, which St Luke refers to, has been a contagious element in carols from many lands. This piece, in that mood, was written by Brien Masters after a visit to Raphael's *Bridgewater Madonna* in the National Gallery of Scotland.

28. This round by Walter Braithwaite is great fun to sing. Without overdoing it, accentuation on the notes shown will help give the effect of peals of bells. The words are by Eileen Hutchins.

29. Apart from being a good vocal rollick, this affords a fine example of a tonic pedal, in the long held top note of the third line. This is beautifully offset by the identical rhythm of the first two lines, allowing the piece to canter along effortlessly.

30. This is the opening song of Schubert's song cycle

"Die schöne Müllerin" of 1823-24. It has the air of the journeyman about it. The suggested recorder asides and introduction are intended to give an experience of Schubert's unfailing sense of proportion in his songs, between accompaniment — which was originally piano — and vocal line.

31. The third note of this song gives the melody a unique uplift as if major is about to emerge from minor. In this way it expresses those unmistakable assurances of the forthcoming spring that are revealed through the appearance of the first aconites and snowdrops, or hazel catkins and greening larches. The words are by J.M.C. Crumm.

32. This charming song seems to breathe the very air of excitement of a large colony of gulls or terns ledged at nesting time above the breakers, the elements mingling joyously in a symphony of regeneration.

33. The interweaving of religion and dance has very ancient origins. Verses from the version of these words that appeared in Sandys in 1833 have been added to (for school assemblies and other occasions) in order to strengthen the elements of resurrection in the story.

34. The eucalyptus, the "gum-tree" referred to in this song, survives incredible periods of drought in the Australian bush. It gives character to the landscape and offers sustenance to insects, birds and the koala bear, popularly thought of as clinging to the smooth trunk, munching. The kookaburra bird is part of the same scene.

35. The words of this Finnish melody are by Catherine van Alphen.

36. A traditional song that children love acting.

37. St Patrick's faith, like a spiritual rock upon which so many have found sure ground, is boldly stated here both in the translation of his words and in the old Irish melody. A full estimation of the contribution of Celtic Christianity to the cultural life of Europe is coming to light by degrees.

38. Schubert is known to have had a very intimate connection with the mood of nature at sunset. This is expressed potently yet with reserve in this *Lied*, "Am Abendrot".

39. This round by Tom Scratchley is enjoyably relaxing if sung in four parts, the fourth line being clapped only, or played with a percussion instrument.

40. Vaughan Williams wrote the music, "Sine Nomine" specially for this hymn.

41. Cecil Harwood was one of the pioneers of the Waldorf movement when it crossed the Channel and came into the English-speaking world. He was an associate both of C.S. Lewis and of Owen Barfield. He particularly admired the melody "Sine Nomine" by

Vaughan Williams whom he also knew personally. His poem, not only in its culminating "Alleluia", but in its whole-hearted and magnanimous gesture towards Creation, was inspired by this melody.

42. The melody of this song is by Michael Wilson whose work with Goethe's theory of colour has become widely known. Formerly an outstanding violinist, he often wrote melodies that could be sung in unsophisticated circumstances. This song was written for a school production of a Norse play about Iduna, the guardian of the apples which were stolen from her. The words are by Eileen Hutchins.

43. The brightness of the bugle tone finds musical expression in the fanfare-like phrase with which this round opens.

44. Thomas Ken became Bishop of Bath and Wells in 1684. These words and those of his "Awake my soul, and with the sun" have accompanied millions of people as they have crossed the threshold of sleep, morning and evening. Thomas Tallis' famous canon first appeared in 1561 in connection with Psalm 67. He was born about five years before Henry VIII's accession in 1509, and is regarded as one of the fathers of English Renaissance style.

45. Whitsuntide is a concept for the older child. Yet the primary teacher may not wish to let it go unnoticed. This round incorporates a few simple images that later can be evolved into relevant concepts.

Age 10-11 (Class 5)

46. This lusty Danish folk tune associated with harvest has all the character of a dance rhythm.

47. The virtual imperceptibility of the 2/4 bar is remarkable in this piece even as it is sung through as a single voice. As a canon, the timelessness of the music is even more pronounced.

48. The traditional manner of singing a Gujarati Bhajan is slowly at first; repeat faster, and still faster the third time; then finally slowing right down the fourth time. A drum and Indian cymbals can be added as "time-keepers".
O Lord, your name I hear in every place, In the sky, breeze and forest;
In the garden and at the "khal-khal" sound of the stream, I hear your song.

49. This ancient Sanskrit chant is an invocation to the light of lights.

50. There are many references to the combustibility of the ash, even when green. Both words and music - originate from the work of Margaret Bennell, founder of Wynstones School and Hawkwood College.

51. The superbly lyrical quality of sacred Renaissance music as evidenced in settings of the mass and motets,

here finds simple expression in this round attributed to Pope Clemens.

52. In most classes there are pupils who can play orchestral instruments. This ostinato could be played by a stranger to the cello by using the open C and G strings, an octave below the notes printed.

53. It is difficult to bring an experience of counterpoint to younger children. In this round, with careful counting, this can be overcome, the beautiful flow of discord and resolution carrying the music forward in dignified procession.

54. Logging or lumbering is common to all tundra regions. And treacherous as well as elating it can be. From forest to pulp mill is a fascinating sequence of events. Skidders get the logs down to the rivers, while the swampers are their helpers. Cant hooks are stout wooden levers with a blunt end and a movable metal arm with a spike to grip the logs; jam pikes are long poles to free the logs when they jam in the river.

55. This exceptionally beautiful Northumbrian folk song was often used as an encore (unaccompanied) by the world famous contralto, Kathleen Ferrier.

56. Alexander Carmichael reveals a wealth of culture of the Gaelic people amongst whom his work took him. Selections of his work are published in *The Sun Dances*, and in *New Moon of the Seasons*, which draw attention to a remarkable survival of imaginative consciousness. This finds further expression in the Easter verses made specially for this old Highland melody.

57. This song is in the Phrygian mode, not in C major. It is exceptional in the way its opening phrase bursts straight into the upper octave. J.M. Neale, whose translations of both Latin and Greek are among the finest, held the post of warden of Sackville College, East Grinstead, at the end of his life.

58. This song refers to the picturesque region of Ayrshire in south-west Scotland associated with Robert Burns. The Doon Valley is famed for its bridge, traditionally the bridge referred to in "Tam o' Shanter".

59. It was Martin Shaw's conception to set Matthew Arnold's version of St Francis' testimony of life in this way, using a Parisian tone as the starting point. The note values should be taken as an approximation, particularly the breves (‖◉‖) which indicate that they should continue long enough for the relevant words to be chanted at a measured speed.

60. In the best tradition of English rounds, vigorously 'tuneful.

61. Sung by Orpheus at the moment that he loses Eurydice on his return from the netherworld, this aria (here abridged to an A-B-A form) comes at one of the most poignant moments in operatic history. Gluck's

masterpiece rises to the occasion in splendid style and in such a way that the melody can be very fully sampled without accompaniment, even in the pregnantly dramatic rests. First produced in Vienna in 1762.

62. The good-natured community feeling that can be felt when people get together to sing, bubbles through this short round despite its minor key. Emphasis should be given to the recurring syncopation (♪♪).

63. In many northern European countries, particularly the former Estonia and Latvia, the summer solstice festivities focused on the all-night midsummer fires.

64. Nonsense, riddle, or double Dutch? Songs in this vein are found in more than one folk song tradition, in one form or another.

65. This piece became the traditional opening song for the first Glee Club which was founded in London in 1790. In jovial mood the members of the Club gathered for an evening's singing of glees (or part-songs).

66. This is attributed to Mozart. Strictly, it is a musical canon and not a round, that is, the second part enters before the first phrase is complete. It is much more difficult to compose, especially achieving at the same time such a natural melody as this one.

67. This immortal melody springs from the very soil of English folk music. It is worth making an effort to get the accidentals exact. In his *Sir John in Love*, Vaughan Williams used this melody with particular aptness, thus bringing together the most popular of English melodies with (in some ways) the most popular of Shakespearean characters, Falstaff. The present phase of the tune's popularity is connected with the fact that it is used as a New Year carol with words that were published in 1642.

Age 11-12 (Class 6)

68. Michael Rose, who wrote this song, is a founder teacher of the York Rudolf Steiner School.

69. Round writing was a popular pastime among classical composers, as often as not for friends to sing. Beethoven put some of his particular brand of wit into his rounds. This one is written by a composer he particularly admired.

70. This translation reflects something of the original meaning of the words of the angel to the shepherds in St Luke's Gospel.

71. A popular example of the genre of the sea-songs recalling the empire-building days of the past when the merchant navy played an important role in the economic life of many European nations.

72. Derived from a thirteenth century dance: the estampie. The melody is in the lower part. Often dances consisted only of a melody. This version could be sung supported by a percussion instrument.

73. Tennyson's sure-handed mastery of poetic form is exemplified here in his taking up a familiar metre but with the rhyming pattern *a-b-b-a*. This helps the mood of New Year ring forth.

74. A typical song for a mountain hike in the Black Forest in southern Germany.

75. *Der Freischütz*, produced in Berlin in 1821, was virtually a turning point in the development of romantic opera. Alongside a spate of settings of Goethe's *Faust*, it is a popular example of the obsession with the supernatural of the time, that often took on grotesque form. This huntsman's "chorus" also illustrates the love of the extensive forests spread over large regions of Germany.

76. Loewe, who composed this three-part song (slightly adapted here), had an exceptional voice, giving song recitals up and down Europe. He was famed for his ballads.

77. This is a particularly vigorous round of Haydn's. The words were written specially to bring out the different facets of the music.

78. In the Middle Ages saintly and sacred relics were among the most treasured possessions of the monasteries. This chant, printed to give an impression of early notation, is associated with the convent at Poitiers, France, where a fragment of the True Cross brought there by Queen Radegund was held. The first verse is given in Latin and in the standard translation: some teachers may wish to use both alongside a study of the period. A further verse has been added for this edition to facilitate closer reference to the legend.

79. This is an example of the finest folk-poetry.

80. This extremely beautiful round is ascribed to Orlando di Lasso, one of the geniuses of Renaissance music. Although, as a round, this music can be experienced as a progression of harmonies, it belongs to an era when music was conceived polyphonically. Polyphony places the emphasis on to the (horizontal) melodic line, the harmony being secondary.

81. This Mixoladian Scottish folk tune (pitched low) combined with what might be described as a folk passion was used by G.R. Woodward in 1924. It must surely be a coincidence that the tune was called "Put the Gown upon the Bishop"! Unlike Bosch and some of the northern European painters who presented the *harshness* of the events of Golgotha, Woodward merely emphasises their incredulity.

82. When the snow melts on the lower Alpine shoulders, spring rites celebrating the return to the heights were part of daily life in all country districts. This is a German song used in some of the festivities,

as animals were taken again to the pastures for the new season.

83. This round is particularly buoyant if the bars that start with a crochet rest are well handled.

84. The richness, mellowness, and serenity of the Italian landscape at eventide is here expressed in a simple but telling melody, arranged in three parts.

85. Addison's metrical version of Psalm 23 is here combined with a melody attributed to Haydn. The composer's masterly handling of the wide intervals needs matching by the singers. Here one experiences the very peaks of classical melody.

86. A glimpse through Purcell's musical telescope of seventeenth century social life for the man in the street.

87. In 1790 Mozart's folk opera *The Magic Flute* made its first and undying impression on the Viennese and on the world. This is one of the trios sung by the three genii on one of their appearances at a crucial moment in the story. This English version seeks to give expression to the relevance of the story beyond mere pantomime — a view often held by critics.

88. Anne, Duchess of Brittany, became Queen of France, clogs 'n all (*les sabots de bois*). This song recounts how this was prophesied when she was handed a sprig of verbena at the gates of Rennes and told that if it flowered (which it did) she would become Queen. The story is here contained within ten lines, plus intervening refrain, making five verses in all. The original form was: Verse 1: Line 1, repeated, Line 2, Chorus; Verse 2: Line 2, repeated, line 3, Chorus, and so on.

89. The Khirghiz and other tribes stand behind the long Hungarian tradition of excellent horsemanship. This exciting canon can be performed simply in two parts, the second entering comfortably after one bar, or, as further developed, depending on the class's ability to tackle the increasing complexity.

Age 12 upwards (Classes 7 & 8)

90. This unusual chant-like song expresses the Celt's strong connection with and reliance upon the supernatural world, in this case also raised to imaginative realms.

91. The chromatically widening intervals with which Haydn opens this round offer a challenge to the singer.

92. This ostinato is designed to be sung antiphonally, that is, by the lower voices dividing into two, the second group taking over (as indicated) while the first group completes the last note. This effect can be enhanced by placing the groups some distance apart. It is particularly effective in a handsomely proportioned stair-well!

93. One of the deeply moving incidents of musical history was when John Blow made way for his young pupil, Henry Purcell, as organist of Westminster Abbey. This bustling round of Purcell's points a moral in a way that was in vogue at the turn of the seventeenth century.

94. There are many incidents in the biography of Martin Luther that attest to the whole-hearted way in which he embraced his cause. Artistically this was expressed first and foremost in the verses and chorale melodies that he wrote for the new Protestant congregations to sing in the vernacular. This one expresses the staunch attitude widely held towards the Reformed faith.

95. This melody contains an inner vigour by virtue of the slurring within the musical phrases. It is typical of the trimphant inner certainty expressed in Bach's work, bearing, as it does, the unmistakable hallmark of the Lutheran Reformation.

96. One of the supreme moments in Dutch history was its emancipation from the political yolk of Spain. This was in no small measure due to the tenacity of the Dutch "Sea-beggars". They epitomize the nation's connection with the ocean, and their relentless fortitude as individuals.

97. Thomas Campion, physician, poet, and composer, published this song in 1613. Perhaps it is best imagined in connection with the sound of the lute. The fact that words and music come from the same pen with such perfect union gives the song exceptional calm and inner radiance.

98. This ancient chant should be performed without *having* to count the (for the West) unusual timing too metronomically.

99. One of the city of Lincoln's claims to fame is undoubtedly its "Angel Choir", named after the magnificent medieval carving of angels on the spandrel of the triforium arcade, the building of which commenced in 1256. It is perhaps less known that William Byrd was organist here at the outset of his career. Later, at the Chapel Royal, he suffered greatly through his devotion to the older faith.

100. This carol derives from Polish folk tradition. Its rhythmic vigour and strident intervals need confident handling.

101. This setting of Tchaikovsky appeared in 1883 in a book of songs for youth. There is an inner drama in the words (originally Russian by Plechtcheev), which the composer has encapsulated. His full harmony may be found in the *Oxford Book of Carols* (No. 197). An average class orchestra can easily tackle a straightforward arrangement of it, with a group holding the melodic line.

102. This song has been transcribed directly from Bolivian oral tradition. The roots of the language go

back to pre-Inca times in South America. It should bustle along quite quickly with the air of gossiping women, particularly in the last verse which can be sung with a cat-that-licked-the cream- smile and a wagging of the tip of the tongue.

103. Brittany has many associations, amongst them are the sea, and the standing stones — sharp contrasts in many ways. The Birth at the midnight hour within the cave seems to arise naturally out of such a setting.

104. This appeared in the collection of *Russian National Songs* that Nicholas Rimsky-Korsakov brought out in 1877. The words of the chorus are those used in parts of Russia as an Easter greeting.

105. Breughel's famous picture of Flemish peasants at a wedding dance inspired these words. Apart from the tricky, unexpected rests that are so typical of Haydn's musical humour, one can really let go in a relaxed mood of village merriment.

106. This is the traditional Welsh tune "Ar hyd y nos", here with the traditional words, but also long connected with the beautiful vesper "God that Madest Earth and Heaven". The melody is in the bass stave.

107. This fourteenth-century piece shines like a musical beacon from the late Middle Ages and is one of the treasures that has come down from Chaucer's times. The slight effort needed to familiarize the pupils with the original language is always richly rewarded.

108. This Israeli song is a greeting and farewell, meaning "Farewell friends, till we meet again." Shalom also means "peace".

Index to titles and *first lines*